BRAZIL
A CHRONOLOGY AND FACT BOOK

1488 -1973

Compiled and Edited by
RUSSELL H. FITZGIBBON

1974
OCEANA PUBLICATIONS, INC
Dobbs Ferry, New York

Library of Congress Cataloging in Publication Data

Fitzgibbon, Russell Humke, 1902-
    Brazil: a chronology and fact book, 1488-1973.

    (World chronology series)
    Bibliography: p.
    1. Brazil--History--Sources. 2. Brazil--History--
Chronology. I. Title.
F2521. F55   981   73-17058
ISBN 0-379-16309-8

Manufactured in the United States of America

TABLE OF CONTENTS

EDITOR'S FOREWORD

Brazil, as the eminent author of a book several years ago characterized it in his subtitle, is "the infinite country." Fifth largest country in
the world, it is many things: it is the great drought-stricken area in the
northeast and it is rain forest; it is the world's mightiest river and it the
vast sertões or hinterland areas, a seemingly permanent frontier; it is the
politically sophisticated middle and upper classes of the cities and it is the
wholly politically inarticulate interior; it is the loveliness of much of Rio
de Janeiro or the bold, futuristic Brasilia and it is the stark favelas on the
hillsides above the large cities.

Perhaps the most obvious and impressive fact about Brazil is its sheer
size, 3,286,478 square miles. The single country includes 49 percent of
the area of South America, 42 percent of that of all Latin America. As is
true of many Latin American countries, effective Brazil is much smaller
than the whole area. Three-tenths of the land area -- Minas Gerais and the
states south, plus a thin coastal strip running north to slightly beyond the
Hump -- contain about nine-tenths of the population and the important economic, cultural, and political centers.

The Northeast, as the scene of recurrent droughts, some of them of
several years' duration, has been an economic and hence a political problem. Brazil's North, generally equated with Amazonia, has in the past en-
gendered a good deal of wishful thinking, as one of the later documents am-
ply illustrates. Growing knowledge has diminished the roseate hopes earlier pinned on the area. The West is a magnet which still rouses the opti-
mism of many Brazilians, as is evidenced in part by the expenditure of hun-
dreds of millions of dollars to establish Brazil's new capital in the area.

Brazil doubtless deserves the label of "melting pot" more than does the
United States. The chief early components of the population were the Indians, Portuguese, and Negroes. Heavy immigration in the nineteenth and
twentieth centuries added millions of Italians, Portuguese, Spaniards, Germans, Poles, Japanese, and many other nationalities so that, especially in
the south and in the cities, the nationalistic mix was extremely varied. A
United Nations breakdown in 1950 placed the Negro fraction at about one-
tenth, the white at about three-fifths, and the mixed at about one-fourth,
but, as is always true, any ethnic statistics must always be viewed cautiously.

In political terms Brazil long enjoyed a reputation for tolerance and
accommodation and democracy despite the fact that (aside from Canada) it
was for many years the New World's only monarchy. In the last century,
however, militarism and military activity in politics have played more of
a role, surfacing, it is true, more at certain times than at others. Especially since 1964 the army has been front and center and the traditional
democratic processes and attitudes have suffered correspondingly. Some

would view this as bad, others as good, but all would probably agree that the customary temper and tempo of Brazilian political life were thereby profoundly affected. In a sense the great country is trying to catch up with and adjust to the intricate and sometimes terrible pressures of the second half of the twentieth century.

Here, then, is Brazil, the infinite country. Its problems seem infinite but its promise may also be infinite.

Russell H. Fitzgibbon
Professor Emeritus
University of California
Santa Barbara

CHRONOLOGY

1488   The French later claimed that a voyage by Jean Cousin in 1488 resulted in the discovery of Brazil. They could not, however, offer any documentary proof of such discovery and it is almost wholly discredited.

1493   May 4. Pope Alexander VI, in order to settle conflicting claims between the two important Catholic powers, Spain and Portugal, to newly discovered lands, issued two papal bulls allotting to Spain all new discoveries west of an imaginary line (the "Line of Demarcation") drawn from pole to pole 100 leagues west of the Azores in the Atlantic, and to Portugal all new lands east of such a line. Although not then known, this would have given Portugal merely the tip of eastern Brazil.

1494   June 7. Since Portugal considered the Demarcation line unsatisfactory, its king managed to obtain from the Spanish a revision of the line in the Treaty of Tordesillas which moved the line to 370 leagues west of the Cape Verde Islands. The line as revised passed approximately through the mouth of the Amazon River. The treaty provided that a joint expedition should sail within 10 months to survey the line but this was not carried out.

1497   Vasco da Gama climaxed a brilliant century of Portuguese exploration, in which ship captains under the encouragement of Prince Henry the Navigator had progressively moved down the West African coast, by rounding Cape Horn at the southern extremity of Africa and reaching India where he found fabulous wealth, especially in spices, for Portugal. The great Indian wealth dulled and postponed Portuguese interest in Brazil. Part of the vagueness of the territorial claims of the time was caused by the continuing policy of secretiveness about Portuguese discoveries followed by the government of that country.

1498   Some Brazilians claim that Duarte Pacheco Pereira, sailing on orders of the Portuguese king, actually discovered Brazil in this year. The claim is, however, generally rejected.

1500   March 8. Pedro Alvares Cabral sailed from the Tagus River in Portugal in command of a fleet of 13 vessels and 1,200 men, ostensibly bound for India. He sailed far to the west to avoid unfavorable winds.

April 22. Cabral's fleet sighted land in what is now
Brazil. The commander landed, had a large cross erected,
and claimed the land (he took it to be an island) for the
Portuguese crown. He spent about a week exploring the
coast for several miles, sent one vessel back to Portugal
with an account of his discoveries, and then sailed on to
Asia where he laid the foundations for a long-lived and
vastly prosperous Portuguese colonial empire in India.

There still is considerable dispute over whether Cabral's
discovery, which formed the basis of the later huge
Portuguese colony of Brazil, was truly accidental, as he
claimed. Winds on the voyage were not actually unfavorable; Vasco da Gama's navigator on his 1497 voyage accompanied Cabral and, some historians believe, must
have known that so extensive a "detour" was unnecessary.
At any rate, Cabral's claim gave Portugal entree into the
New World.

Cabral named the new land the Island of Vera Cruz but it
was also known as the Province or Land of Vera Cruz.
These names, however, did not catch on. When early
ships returned to Portugal with a considerable cargo of
logs from coastal forests containing a valuable red dye
"equal to that known in Europe as Brazil" that word itself
was very soon popularly applied to the whole country.

1501   The Portuguese crown sent an expedition of three ships
to explore the Brazilian coast south of Natal. Amerigo
Vespucci, who reported on the expedition (and whose name
was later given to the two continents of the New World),
described the Brazilian coast in glowing terms: "If there
is a Paradise anywhere on earth, it cannot be very far
from here."

1503   Fernão de Noronha, holder of a royal concession to ex-
ploit the wealth in brazilwood, sent ships to cut logs and
bring them back to Europe. The trade became very
lucrative as the value of the dye was quickly recognized
by the new European textile industries. By the end of the
16th century almost 100 ships per year were sailing from
Brazil to Portugal with cargoes of the dyewood.

1516   French activity, stimulated by a wish to cut in on the
profitable Portuguese trade in dyewood, led to the dispatch
of a small fleet by King João III with orders to scuttle all

hostile ships found in Brazilian waters. Many French
vessels were sunk by the Portuguese ships and raids by
the French were greatly reduced but not eliminated.
France, although a strongly Catholic country, had never
recognized the validity of the Line of Demarcation or the
Treaty of Tordesillas, and assumed that it could hold
what it could win in the New World. Hence, by 1530 it
was an open question as to whether Brazil would remain a
Portuguese possession or fall to French hands.

1521   A colonist planted sugar cane in what became the province
of Pernambuco, thus laying the foundation for the Brazilian
economy for two centuries to come.

1526   The Portuguese dispatched another small fleet to try to
contain French activity in Brazil. It was largely unsuccessful.

1530   The Portuguese crown determined on a major policy reversal for Brazil: colonization rather than merely
trading. The result was the dispatch of a major expedition under Martim Affonso de Souza with five ships, some
400 sailors and colonists, and quantities of plants, seeds,
and domestic animals. This marked the true beginning
of Brazilian development as something more than simply
a trading outpost.

Substitution of early Portuguese indifference to its great
colony by active concern for its future is explainable in
terms of four factors: realization of the great profits to
be gained from dyewood exploitation, alarm over the continuing and expanding French interest in gaining a Brazilian
foothold (King Francis I of France had declared that he
"had never seen a clause in the last will of Adam conceding exclusive control" to the kings of Portugal and Spain),
growing Portuguese fear over Spanish ambitions in the
New World and jealousy of the vast wealth Spain had found
in Mexico and Peru, and the diminishing Portuguese trade
with India.

1532   Martim Affonso founded the town of São Vicente near the
present city of Santos in southern Brazil. It was the first
permanent settlement in Brazil.

1533   Brazil's first sugar mill was set up in the vicinity of São
Vicente. In the highlands back of São Vicente Martim

Affonso founded a village, Piratininga, which later became
the great city of São Paulo. One of his directives--unful-
filled--was for the organization of an expedition "against
the Inca," i.e., against the fabulously wealthy west-coast
Spanish colony of Peru.

The explorations of Martim Affonso, covering some
3,000 miles up and down the coast of Brazil, vastly increased Portuguese knowledge of its sprawling colony and
whetted Portuguese commitment to more systematic development. Establishment of Portuguese footholds in both
the north, near present-day Bahia, and the south, at modern
São Paulo, was facilitated by discovery of shipwrecked
Portuguese sailors who had polygamously mated with
natives and established huge families of mixed-blood off-
spring, known in Brazil as mamelucos rather than by the
Spanish term mestizos. In the south the mamelucos became the ancestors of the aggressive, restless, and
venturesome paulistas, as the inhabitants of the province
(and later the state) of São Paulo were called. The
paulistas were responsible for much of the later westward
expansion of Brazilian territory, far beyond the limits set
by the Treaty of Tordesillas.

King João III in 1533 began the system of captaincies or
great feudal grants that had proved successful in Madeira
and the Azores. Great estates or fiefs were granted to
crown vassals known as donataries (donatarios) who were
given almost sovereign powers over their grants and responsibility for settlement, exploitation, and development.
In return they were required to pay the crown a part of
taxes and revenues collected. The Brazilian coastline was
divided into sections of 50 leagues, each known as a captaincy. From the terminal points lines were to be drawn
due west to the Tordesillas line. In practice this plan
broke down: where the coastline varied from a north-
south direction (and much of it did) the size of a captaincy
would be correspondingly diminished, and internal lines
hence often departed from an east-west direction; much
of the interior was unexplored, and the Portuguese had
little respect anyway for a self-imposed limitation to the
confines of the Tordesillas Treaty. As a reward for his
great services Martim Affonso was given a double grant,
i.e., a coastline of 100 leagues in extent, and his brother,
a skillful sailor and able lieutenant of the admiral, received
a grant of 80 leagues.

Of the 12 original grants, only two proved undeniably profitable before the middle of the 16th century: those to Martim Affonso in São Vicente and to Duarte Coelho Pereira in Pernambuco. Nonetheless, the captaincies in several cases gave their names and in general their boundaries to later corresponding provinces and then states.

1548 João III, realizing that, with the exception of the captaincies of São Vicente and Pernambuco, the system of feudal grants was not notably successful, bought back the captaincy of Bahia from its donatary and made it into a crown captaincy. He made the town of Bahia the capital of a new colonial government of Brazil and appointed a number of administrative officials.

1549 João issued a decree strictly limiting the authority of the donataries and establishing the position of governor general for the whole of Brazil. To that post he appointed a Portuguese noble, Tomé de Souza, who had already had a distinguished career in India and Africa.

March 29. The fleet of six ships carrying Tomé de Souza and other officials arrived at Bahia to establish the new order. The governor general was accompanied by six priests headed by Father Manoel de Nóbrega of the recently established order of Jesuits. This was a recognition of the lax state of religious activity in the vast colony. Priests had previously been few in number and often of questionable character. Priestly concern had earlier been almost wholly with the needs of the Portuguese colonists rather than with conversion of the Indians. Between 1549 and 1598, 128 Jesuits went to Brazil. Their missionary zeal left a permanent impress on the colony. Also accompanying the approximately 1,000 colonists and soldiers were some 400 petty criminals who were thus exiled from Portugal.

Tomé de Souza took prompt steps to build a more substantial capital, to send officials to the approximately 15 other Portuguese settlements scattered along the coast in order to correct abuses and tighten administration, and to build more sugar mills and import cattle.

1551 The first steps were taken to create a Catholic diocese in Brazil. The Pope made a permanent grant of ecclesiastical patronage (the authority to appoint high clerical officials) to the Portuguese king.

1553	Tomé de Souza ended his term as governor general and was succeeded by Duarte da Costa.
1555	The French founded a colony at Rio de Janeiro to promote trade with the natives, especially in brazilwood. France had first begun trading along the Brazilian coast in 1504 and had recurrently been a threat to Portuguese domination of the colony. The settlement at Rio, known as Antarctic France, was a menace to the Portuguese for years.
1557	A new and exceptionally able governor general, Mem de Sá, began a 15-year tenure as head of the colony.
1567	Portuguese forces under Mem de Sá were successful in dislodging the French from Rio de Janeiro and establishing their own colony on the magnificent bay.
1570	Father Nóbrega died. His score of years in Brazil succeeded in strongly implanting Catholicism in the colony, although on many later occasions landholders, especially in São Paulo, clashed with Jesuits over practices of forced labor to which they subjected the Indians.
1580	The Portuguese dynasty of Aviz came to an end and King Philip II of Spain, partly by force and partly by bribery, managed to get himself chosen to occupy the Portuguese throne. This united the vast Spanish and Portuguese colonial empires and gave the Spanish control of all of South and most of North America. It resulted in considerable confusion as to where the dividing line between Portuguese and Spanish possessions in South America fell, and Brazilian colonists soon endeavored to push their exploration and settlements farther and farther to the west. The 60-year Spanish occupancy of the Portuguese throne (the "Babylonian captivity" of Portugal) resulted in establishing somewhat similar but not identical administrative agencies in Portuguese and Spanish colonies in South America. The two South American empires were not amalgamated, however.
	By 1580 Brazil had eight firmly established captaincies (not all prosperous, however), a population between 17,000 and 25,000 Portuguese, 18,000 "civilized" Indians, and 14,000 Negro slaves, 60 sugar mills, and a thriving trade in sugar, dyewood, and cotton.

1591   Thomas Cavendish, the English explorer, burned the
            settlement at Santos.

1595   King Philip II reduced the punishment for Indians enslaved
            after capture in war to 10 years of slavery.

1604   A Dutch fleet attacked Bahia.

1605   King Philip III decreed that all Indians, whether converted
            or not, were to be considered free, were not subject to
            forced labor, and must be paid for voluntary work. Strong
            pressures from planters forced modification of this humane
            measure in 1611 and restored enslavement of Indian war
            prisoners. The high mortality among Indian slaves ac-
            celerated importation of African Negro slaves. In time,
            as much as 95 percent of some northern coastal areas
            came to be Negro.

1615   French forces were finally expelled from a settlement in
            Maranhão in the Amazon delta which they had occupied
            for some years.

1621   The Dutch West India Company was established with a
            stated aim of taking over Portuguese possessions in
            Brazil. At an earlier stage the Dutch and Portuguese had
            gotten along amicably but when Portugal was united with
            Spain in 1580 the deep enmity between the Netherlands and
            Spain was then extended by the Dutch to Portugal and its
            vast American colony.

1624   A Dutch West India Company fleet, commanded by Admiral
            Piet Heyn, captured Bahia but had to give it up the follow-
            ing year.

1629   Twenty-one mission villages in the Upper Paraná region
            were raided by a band of 900 paulistas, and some 2,500
            Indians were captured, most of whom were sold into
            slavery.

1630   The Dutch captured Olinda and Recife in the captaincy
            of Pernambuco.

1632   Adherence to the Dutch cause by an able mameluco,
            Domingos Fernandes Calabar, enabled the Dutch to ex-
            tend their coastal dominion in Brazil for almost 1,200
            miles. This seemed far more spectacular at the time
            than their purchase of a small island in New York harbor,
            Manhattan, in 1626.

1636   Spain attempted to send reinforcements to Brazil to de-
            fend the area against the Dutch but Spanish involvements
            in Europe were too serious to permit much defensive ef-
            fort in Brazil and, too, Spanish war vessels were inferior
            to those of the Dutch. Hence, Brazilian defense had to be
            left largely to the colonists themselves. They responded
            with vigor and success and within a few years had con-
            fined the Dutch to a few coastal settlements.

1637   Appointment by the Dutch of Prince John Maurice of
            Nassau as their chief Brazilian administrator introduced
            an able and conciliatory rule into their Brazilian holdings
            and postponed final Portuguese recovery but could not
            stop it permanently. John Maurice ruled Dutch Brazilian
            possessions until 1644.

1640   When the Portuguese threw off the Spanish yoke in
            Portugal a shift in European alliances resulted that an-
            tagonized Brazilians against the Portuguese.

1648   The Dutch hold in Brazil was by this time reduced to
            Recife and its immediate vicinity.

1654   The Dutch withdrew all their colonists and equipment
            from Pernambuco to the West Indies.

1676   Bahia became the seat of Brazil's first archbishop.

1680   The Portuguese, aided by paulistas, established a colony
            at Sacramento on the left bank of the Plata River.

1693   The "gold rush" to Minas Gerais (the name means
            General Mines) began. Agriculture suffered greatly as
            sugar planters abandoned their estates and hastened to
            the mines with their slaves. Cotton raising also suffered
            (though the effects were not felt immediately) because of
            the invention of Eli Whitney's cotton gin which greatly
            stimulated later United States production.

1697   Paulistas, after several unsuccessful efforts, finally
            destroyed the "Republic of Palmares," a well organized
            community of some 20,000 escaped Negro slaves that
            had been set up in the interior of Brazil.

1711   By this time an estimated 30,000 men were engaged in
            mining in Minas Gerais.

1720   The province of Minas Gerais was made a captaincy.

1727   Coffee growing was introduced into Brazil from French
                Guiana. By 1770 it had reached Rio de Janeiro.

1729   A "diamond rush" to Minas Gerais further emphasized
                the great mineral value of that area. A few diamonds
                had been found as early as 1723 but their nature was not
                then recognized. If gold and diamonds had been found a
                century earlier in Minas Gerais it is questionable whether
                the Portuguese hold on Brazil could have been maintained
                against Dutch and/or French efforts to win the colony.

1750   October 5. The Spanish-Portuguese boundary in South
                America established by the Treaty of Tordesillas, a line
                which had never been surveyed or respected, was of-
                ficially abandoned by a new combination of principles
                embodied in the Treaty of Madrid. The new treaty re-
                cognized ownership based on occupation of land and also
                sought to make use of natural boundaries. Portuguese
                were thus confirmed in title to vast lands beyond the
                Tordesillas line.

                A new Portuguese king, José, appointed Sebastião José
                de Carvalho e Mello, better known as the marquis of
                Pombal, as secretary of state for foreign affairs and war.
                Within a short time he had gained complete ascendancy
                over the king and was himself virtual ruler of Portugal
                and its empire until his dismissal just after the king's
                death in 1777. He considerably tightened Portuguese
                administration in Brazil, where some of his actions
                brought him into conflict with the Jesuits who felt he was
                infringing their long-established prerogatives of control
                over Indian communities.

1755   After a devastating earthquake in Lisbon, Pombal tenta-
                tively advanced a plan that Portugal should abandon
                Europe and create a powerful empire in Brazil. Nothing
                then came of the idea.

1759   September. After five years of growing controversy with
                the Jesuits, Pombal issued an order expelling them from
                all Portuguese dominions, including Brazil.

1763   The seat of the viceroy of Brazil was moved to Rio de
                Janeiro.

1777   The Treaty of San Ildefonso further modified the Portuguese-
            Spanish South American boundary in favor of Brazil.

1789   Discontent with Portuguese authorities led to a revolt in
            Minas Gerais, initiated by members of the intellectual
            elite of the area. It was led by Joaquim José da Silva
            Xavier, better known by his nickname of Tiradentes
            ("Tooth-puller"). The revolt and resulting trials of the
            leaders dragged on for more than two years.

1792   April 21. Tiradentes was hanged for his part in the revolt,
            the only leader to suffer capital punishment. Others
            were exiled or imprisoned.

1795   The Treaty of Basle left Portugal abandoned by its former
            European allies and in opposition to both France and Spain.
            This brought the future of Brazil more into speculation.

1801   Brazilians attacked Spanish forces in the Plata region and
            captured the settlement at Missões. They thus pushed
            the southern boundary of Brazil to the Chuí River, its
            present location. The Treaty of Badajós, later in the
            year, recognized this expansion.

1807   November 29. As a consequence of Napoleon's invasion
            of Spain and Portugal in an effort to block off the English,
            with whom he was having a titanic struggle for mastery
            of Europe, from all access to the Continent, the Portu-
            guese regent, João VI, acting for his insane queen mother,
            sailed from the Tagus River with the entire royal court
            of more than 1,000, and retainers, archives, and treasure,
            for Brazil, in order to escape the French capture that
            was facing King Ferdinand of Spain. The departure had
            long been planned in case French pressure should become
            too great. A French army entered Lisbon unopposed the
            following day.

1808   January. After a stormy voyage the English-convoyed
            Portuguese fleet arrived in Bahia to complete transference
            of the Portuguese court to the New World. Reception of
            the royal court by Bahia was friendly--it was a matter of
            pride that Brazil should now become the center of the
            Portuguese empire. But the welcome soon wore thin as
            the arrogance and demanding attitude of many of the
            courtiers increasingly antagonized the Brazilians. After
            resting from the strenuous voyage for a few weeks the

court sailed south for Rio de Janeiro, the capital.

Brazil at this time represented more promise than achieve-
ment. Its population of above 3,000,000 was largely illiterate and politically inarticulate. About two-thirds of
the inhabitants were slaves and many others were little
advanced beyond that status. The sprawling colony was
culturally retarded: there were few schools or books and
no universities. The Church provided a partially unifying
force but the earlier expulsion of the Jesuits had decreased
its impact. Against that negative side, Brazil felt stirrings
of nationalism based both on its own successful efforts in
earlier expelling the Dutch and on the expansionist activities of the paulista bandeirantes (those who went on far-
flung exploring and slave-raiding expeditions into the remote
interior).

Regent João reacted very favorably to Brazil, quite in con-
trast to his haughty wife, Carlota Joaquina. The regent
opened Brazilian ports to world trade, with special concessions to the British; he encouraged immigration and
development of industry; he established a national bank,
a printing press and national library, a medical school
and a military academy. Results of all of the innovations
were thoroughly yeasty so far as Brazilian psychology was
concerned. The colony's economy was similarly accelerated.

1815   January 16. João issued a decree raising Brazil to the
            status of a separate kingdom, greatly to the pleasure of
            Brazilians but to the considerable dismay of leaders in the
            mother country.

1816   March. The insane Queen María I, mother of João, died
            and was succeeded by her son as João VI, king of the
            United Kingdom of Portugal, Brazil, and the Algarves (the
            last-mentioned was the southernmost province of Portugal,
            which for centuries had maintained a fiction of autonomy).
            This new status led to additional pomp, especially for
            Rio de Janeiro. Portuguese leaders tried to exert pressure
            on João to return to Portugal but he refused, partly because
            he suspected Carlota Joaquina of designs to set herself up
            as queen of an independent Brazilian kingdom. She also
            allegedly intrigued with monarchist elements in Buenos
            Aires to get herself chosen ruler of a reunited La Plata
            region, a revival of the old Spanish viceroyalty of that name.

Brazil annexed the Banda Oriental (the "East Bank" of the
Uruguay River; what is modern Uruguay) as part of the
long-lived feud between Portugal and Spain, and later between Brazil and Argentina, over that buffer area. Brazilian
possession, however, did not become permanent, although
it resulted in an early war between Brazil and Argentina
over possession of the area. Partly because of the rebellion of patriotic Uruguayans and partly because of
British diplomatic pressure, Uruguay became an independent republic in the 1820's.

1817   Growing restlessness by Brazilians over the arrogance of
Portuguese courtiers and the extravagance of the regime
expressed itself in a temporarily serious revolt in
Pernambuco. It was quickly crushed and its leaders were
hanged but it added to the friction between Brazilians and
Portuguese.

1820   A liberal revolt in Portugal deposed the regent and convened a parliament which adopted a constitution closely
patterned after an earlier Liberal Spanish constitution.
The new government, wishing to hold Brazil, condemned
the opening of Brazilian ports, revoked many of João's
orders for Brazil, and instructed Brazilian provinces and
Portuguese officers in his Brazilian forces to ignore his
commands. Revolutionary activity occurred in Bahia and
Pará. Fearing he might lose both Brazilian and Portuguese
crowns, João, under British urging, determined to return
to Portugal.

1821   April 26. João and some 3,000 of his court sailed for
Portugal. The king wept at leaving Brazil but Carlota was
ostentatiously happy over returning to Portugal. João took
with him all the gold in the Brazilian treasury. He left
his 23-year-old son Pedro as regent and, anticipating a
likely complete split between Portugal and her colony, advised Pedro: "If Brazil demands independence, grant it,
but put the crown on your own head." Pedro was handsome,
athletic, impulsive, sensual, generous, clever, intel-
ligent, realistic, and rude.

The Portuguese parliament soon sent Pedro express orders
to return to Portugal, ostensibly to complete his education.
Delegations from various cities implored him to stay in
Brazil.

1822   January 9. Pedro informed the municipality of Rio de Janeiro that he would remain in Brazil. This caused a mutiny by the Portuguese garrison of 1, 600 troops stationed in Rio de Janeiro, who thus tried to force the return of Pedro to Portugal.

January 16. In a new ministry organized in Brazil José Bonifacio de Andrada e Silva, an eminent Brazilian later known as the Patriarch of Brazilian Independence, became the guiding spirit. He channeled the growing sentiment for breaking away from the mother country.

May 13. Pedro accepted the title "Perpetual Defender of Brazil" which a popular movement had proposed he should be granted.

September 7. A further peremptory order from the Portuguese authorities that Pedro must return to Portugal was taken by couriers from Rio de Janeiro to the regent who was traveling in São Paulo. They reached him on the banks of a small stream near São Paulo city. Reading the Portuguese dispatches and realizing the nature of the ultimatum, Pedro tore the Portuguese colors from his uniform, waved his hat in the air, and shouted "Independence or Death!" This became known as the grito (cry) of Ypiranga, and September 7 is the accepted date for marking Brazilian independence from Portugal. A Portuguese garrison at Bahia tried to hold out but it and small Portuguese forces elsewhere were ultimately subdued and expelled. Brazilian independence was assured by 1823 and had been achieved almost without bloodshed.

December 1. The regent was crowned as Pedro I, Constitutional Emperor and Perpetual Defender of Brazil.

1823   April 17. A constituent assembly, provided for in 1822, held its first meeting. It was dominated by José Bonifacio de Andrada and his two brothers who by this time were in opposition to the emperor. Members reflected regional antagonisms and the growing friction between patriotic Brazilians and the pro-Portuguese element, which was still strong.

July 2. The last major force of Portuguese troops in Brazil embarked to return to Lisbon.

November 11. Disgusted by the divisions and bitterness of
the assembly, Pedro ordered its dissolution. He promised
at the same time to prepare and grant to the nation a
genuinely liberal constitution. Leaders of the suspended
assembly were exiled. Pedro at once convened a commission of ten Brazilians to draft a new basic law, which they
accomplished by December. It was then submitted to the
various municipal councils for consideration and approval.

1824   March 25. The new constitution was promulgated by the
              emperor. It established a highly centralized executive
              branch and in addition to the three traditional branches or
              "powers" of government (executive, legislative and judi-
              cial) it created and gave to the emperor the "moderative"
              power, making him a sort of balance wheel among the other
              branches and with the provinces.

              May 26. The United States recognized Brazilian independ-
              ence, the first foreign power to do so.

1825   August 29. Great Britain followed suit by recognizing
              Brazilian independence.

1826   March 10. King João of Portugal died. He and his minis-
              ters had made plans for the succession of Emperor Pedro
              to the Portuguese throne but Pedro abandoned his rights to
              that crown and nominated his five-year-old daughter as
              successor to João with the stipulation that she become be-
              trothed to her uncle Miguel.

              By this time Pedro was losing popularity in Brazil. Among
              the causes were the extravagance of the Brazilian court,
              Pedro's favoritism to Portuguese courtiers, a growing
              estrangement from his popular queen, Leopoldina, and
              open maintenance of a mistress, and contemptuous treat-
              ment of cabinet members and deputies in parliament.

1827   Two law schools, at São Paulo and Recife, were founded.
              An astronomical observatory was established at Rio de
              Janeiro.

1828   August 27. Brazil signed a treaty by which the independence
              of Uruguay was recognized and which committed Brazil to
              withdraw her troops from that country. This action added
              to Pedro's unpopularity.

1830   Brazil adopted a new and more systematic criminal code.

                An earlier Brazilian-British treaty provided that importa-
                tion of slaves into Brazil should end in 1830; its provisions
                were not strictly enforced, however.

                By this time the friction between emperor and parliament
                was becoming serious. Pedro exhibited growing aversion
                for the legislature and a greater fondness for the military.
                His reactions to crises appeared increasingly emotional
                and even passionate.

1831   April 7. The political situation rapidly deteriorated early
                in the year and on April 7 Pedro signed an act of abdication
                and soon thereafter sailed with his family for Portugal,
                where he died in 1834. As successor he named his five-
                year-old son, Pedro de Alcântara. Brazil would finally
                have a ruler who was Brazilian both by birth and spirit.

                June 17. A regency of three members was set up to rule
                during Pedro II's minority. The regency was marked by
                considerable storm and stress caused by fears of a pos-
                sible return of absolutism to Brazil, civil disturbances and
                secessionist threats, slave revolts, and other divisive
                factors.

1832   October 12. Preliminary legislation passed parliament
                looking toward decentralizing political organization, per-
                haps even establishing a federation.

1833   A military revolt occurred in Minas Gerais but was quelled.
                Riots and disturbances continued sporadically in numerous
                provinces throughout most of the decade.

1834   August 12. Parliament completed the constitutional reform
                initiated in 1832 by adopting the Additional Act of amend-
                ment to the constitution. This series of amendments
                abolished the council of state, provided for a single regent,
                instead of three, to govern during the emperor's minority,
                and created provincial legislatures with considerable
                autonomy.

                September 24. The death of Emperor Pedro I in Portugal
                brought an automatic end to the fear of many Brazilians
                that he might be restored to rule in that country and led

gradually to a lessening of tension in public life. A conservative party slowly crystallized and occupied a middle
ground between autocratic reaction and exaggerated federalism.

1835   April 7. Father Diogo Antônio Feijó, previously minister
            of justice, was elected as the single regent for a four-year
            term; he assumed office October 12. He was energetic and
            reflected a desire for law and order, but by the time he
            took office he had lost much of his earlier drive.

1836   Rebellion in the southernmost province of Rio Grande do
            Sul veered toward secession but its proponents would have
            been satisfied with Brazilian federalism. Peace was not
            concluded in the south until 1845.

1837   September 19. Feijó, frustrated by the many internal di-
            visions, especially those in southern Brazil, resigned as
            regent. He was succeeded by Pedro de Araujo Lima.

1840   By this time the political picture in Rio Grande do Sul was
            complicated by the almost chronic interference by the
            Argentine dictator, Juan Manuel de Rosas, in Uruguayan
            and southern Brazilian affairs.

            April. Because of Brazilian internal divisions and dissen-
            sions a feeling rapidly began to crystallize that the only
            real solution was to declare Pedro of age (even though he
            was only 15) and prevail upon him to assume active rule.

            July 23. Asked by an official delegation to assume the
            imperial power immediately, Pedro replied, "Yes, I wish
            it at once." He then entered upon his functions as ruler.

1841   November 23. The council of state was re-established as
            a check on ill-considered and hasty action by both legis-
            lative and executive branches.

1843   The first steam navigation of the Amazon River occurred.

1850   September 4. Parliament passed a law abolishing the
            slave trade.

1851   The first regular steamship line to Europe began operation.

May 29. Brazil, Uruguay, and two Argentine provinces signed a treaty pledging joint opposition to the Argentine dictator Rosas. He was subsequently defeated in battle early in 1852, which ended his long rule in Argentina.

The Bank of Brazil was founded by the Viscount Mauá.

1852   Brazil's first telegraph line was opened.

1854   Brazil's first railway, about nine miles in length, was built near Rio de Janeiro.

1859   Brazil concluded a treaty with Argentina by which both countries again guaranteed the sovereignty of Uruguay. Nonetheless, repeated raids from Rio Grande do Sul into Uruguayan territory raised Argentine fears of Brazilian imperialistic ambitions.

1860   Independent Brazil first achieved a favorable balance of trade, due to rapidly increasing coffee exports.

1861   Brazil's relations with the United States were strained because of the former country's declaration of neutrality in the American Civil War and the granting of belligerent rights to Confederate vessels.

1863   June. Brazil broke diplomatic relations with Great Britain as the culmination of repeated instances of friction between the two countries. As a consequence Pedro concluded that Brazilian military and naval strength must be increased.

1864   November 11. The megalomaniac dictator of Paraguay, Francisco Solano López, seized a Brazilian steamboat on the Paraguay River. The act was an outgrowth of a complex series of involvements among Paraguay, Brazil, Argentina, and Uruguay and was a reflection of López's ambition to build a larger Paraguay and to dominate the politics of the Plata region.

December. López sent troops to occupy the Brazilian territory of Mato Grosso.

1865   January. López requested Argentine permission to cross her territory to attack the southernmost Brazilian province of Rio Grande do Sul. When the Argentine government refused, López sent Paraguayan troops in anyway and hence

brought Argentina into war as well as Brazil. Brazilian
pressure forced Uruguay also to enter the war against
Paraguay.

May 1. Brazil, Argentine, and Uruguay signed the Treaty
of the Triple Alliance by which they agreed not to lay down
arms until López's power had been destroyed.

June 11. Paraguayan river naval forces were almost
completely destroyed by a Brazilian squadron. A key
part of the Paraguayan army was defeated in battle on
August 17, 1865. Nevertheless, Paraguayan forces managed
to prolong the war until 1870.

1866   December 7. The emperor decreed that after September
7, 1867, navigation on the Amazon River should be free
to merchant ships of all nations.

1869   January 5. Asunción, the Paraguayan capital, was occupied by allied troops, López, however, fled to the
north and continued fighting for more than a year longer.

1870   March 1. López was killed near the Brazilian border.
This virtually ended the Paraguayan War.

June 20. Brazil and Argentina signed a preliminary
treaty of peace. Uruguay adhered to it on August 1, 1870.
Final peace terms were more difficult to reach.

December 3. A number of advanced liberals issued the
so-called Republican Manifesto calling for abolition of
the empire and establishment of a republic. São Paulo
sent the first Republican deputy to parliament in 1876.

1871   September 28. A notable law provided that all children
born of slave mothers should be free. Almost all slave
owners availed themselves of a provision in the law that
they might make free use of the services of such children
to the age of 21.

1872   January. Weary of the delays in reaching a final peace
agreement, chiefly caused by Argentina, Brazil signed
with Paraguay four treaties covering different aspects of
a peace settlement. Nonetheless, difficulties of interpretation persisted until 1876. The five years of war had

cost Brazil about $300 million and some 50,000 lives.
The country gained a new sense of national unity and won
some Paraguayan territory.

1873   By this time friction involving the Catholic Church and
        the Masonic order was becoming increasingly embroiled
        in politics. The emperor was a high-ranking Mason.

1874   Immigration began a spectacular upturn. Within the next
        decade and a half over 600,000 immigrants entered Brazil,
        chiefly from Italy, Spain, Germany, and Portugal.

1875   September 17. Amnesty granted by Pedro to imprisoned
        high Church officials temporarily eased relations between
        government and the Church. The period was, however,
        marked by increasing disintegration of the prestige of
        the empire and by growing criticism of the emperor
        himself.

1878   Election of Joaquim Nabuco, a fiery abolitionist, to the
        chamber of deputies, revived discussion of the slavery
        problem and tended to cast it in philosophical and human-
        itarian terms rather than purely economic ones. A bill
        he introduced in 1880 providing for the ending of slavery
        after ten years was defeated. Nabuco then began a long
        propaganda campaign which greatly increased abolitionist
        sentiment in Brazil.

1881   January 9. An electoral reform law provided for direct
        election (instead of the previous indirect method) and
        gave equal rights to all voters; voting, however, was
        still quite restricted.

1884   March 25. The coastal province of Ceará in the north
        officially declared slavery at an end within the province
        On July 10 the province of Amazonas took similar action.

1885   September 28. An act of parliament provided for liberat-
        ing all slaves over the age of 65. This resulted in the
        freeing of 120,000 slaves.

1888   May 13. A parliamentary law provided for the immediate
        and uncompensated emancipation of the remaining slaves.
        This was at once signed and promulgated by the Princess
        Isabel, serving as regent in the absence of her father,

the emperor, in Europe. By the action the great estate
owners were consolidated in opposition to the empire.

1889   June 7. A new ministry assumed power and immediately
faced tremendous problems. Emancipation of the final
600,000 slaves the preceding year, with an estimated consequent loss to the estate owners of $120 million, created
serious economic problems. The military was becoming
increasingly critical of the government, almost rebellious,
Republican sentiment was growing rapidly. The Catholic
Church was greatly disillusioned with the imperial regime.

Although the emperor had consistently supported the army
during the Paraguayan War, and in return had the loyal
support of its older officers, Pedro remained a convinced
pacifist and was uninterested in military trappings and
postures. Younger officers felt that after the war the
army was being downgraded. One of the leaders of this
group was Colonel Benjamin Constant Botelho de Magalhães,
a devoted advocate of establishment of a republic. Constant was also a follower of the French positivist phi-
losopher August Comte, whose doctrines, eagerly espoused
in various Latin American countries, tended to reject the
"old order" in favor of a new and "scientific" method of
conducting government and economic life.

November 15. A military plot, hatched with great secrecy
by Colonel Constant and close associates, had been
scheduled to culminate in an uprising on November 20 but
earlier rumors that the government planned to arrest
Marshal Manoel Deodoro da Fonseca, a leading army officer, caused the conspirators to advance their plans.
Deodoro* had previously been loyal to the emperor but
Constant finally won him over to the republican cause.
Early on the morning of November 15 army officers ar-
rested the cabinet and later in the day proclaimed a republic. The empire, which had lasted for two-thirds of
a century, had come to an end. Although Pedro had remained personally popular his organized support had
almost completely evaporated. He had progressively
lost the support of the clergy, the great estate owners,
and the military.

---

*Brazilians often refer to their public figures simply by a given name
rather than the surname.

November 16. Marshal Deodoro assumed the provisional presidency of what was proclaimed to be a federated republic until adoption of a formal constitution.

November 17. Emperor Pedro and his family took ship for Portugal. Pedro, already ill with diabetes, died in Paris on December 5, 1891.

December 3. The new government appointed a special commission to prepare a draft constitution for the republic. The commission submitted its draft to the government about six months later.

1890   Almost from the beginning of the republican regime Marshal Deodoro proved an inept administrator. He was personally dignified and honorable but a man of no political experience and of poor judgment in picking advisers. He leaned heavily on army officers, even those just out of military academy. Financial problems continued to be critical.

January 7. The government formally decreed separation of Church and state. The consideration with which the military regime approached this delicate question won approval for the action from the Church hierarchy.

January 29. The United States became the first non-Latin American state to recognize republican Brazil.

September 15. Elections were held for delegates to a constituent convention to consider the revised constitutional draft.

November 15. The constituent assembly began its sessions on the first anniversary of the republican coup d'etat. On the convening of the assembly the marshal had turned over his authority to it but it asked him to remain at the head of the executive branch until it elected a national president and vice-president. Very soon, however, the assembly began to coalesce into two groups, one supporting and the other opposing Deodoro. The marshal resented criticism and friction between him and the assembly grew.

1891   February 24. The new constitution, the first of the re-

public, was adopted. It was chiefly the work of Ruy Barbosa, principal author of the preliminary draft, and reflected
in considerable part the governmental structure of the
United States. The former Brazilian provinces were now
to be known as states and were given substantial autonomy.
Great disparity existed among them, however. The wealth-
iest and most important were São Paulo, Minas Gerais,
Rio de Janeiro, Rio Grande do Sul, Pernambuco, and Bahia,
especially the first three.

February 25. The assembly elected Deodoro constitutional president. A substantial opposition vote for a paulista
civilian, however, betokened the growing antagonism between civilian and military elements.

November 3. Deodoro, indignant over congressional hostility, dissolved both houses of the legislature.

November 23. Revolt against the military government
broke out in Rio Grande do Sul. Pará was on the verge of
revolt and even military and naval units in Rio de Janeiro,
as well as the whole congress and large numbers of civilians, voiced opposition. Greatly shocked by this almost
total loss of support, Deodoro resigned and was succeeded
by the vice-president, Marshal Floriano Peixoto.

1892   January. Armed resistance to the Peixoto government man-
ifested itself, especially in protest against his connivance
in the removal of several opposition state governors. Uprisings were suppressed and a number of generals exiled
or imprisoned.

June. The so-called "federalist revolt" was begun in Rio
Grande do Sul. It obtained some successes in the southern
states, and later allied forces with the revolting naval elements, but was suppressed by June, 1894.

The financial position of the government deteriorated badly
during the year.

1893   September 6. A long anticipated naval revolt broke out.
Army officers were overwhelmingly republican in sentiment but many high naval officers hoped for a restoration
of the monarchy. The admiral heading the revolt ordered
bombardment of Rio de Janeiro by ships stationed in its
harbor but foreign squadrons anchored there threatened to

prevent such an action by force if necessary. The naval opposition was thus largely stalemated. Peixoto at great cost began purchasing naval vessels abroad and training sailors to man them.

1894   March 13. The new fleet was prepared to engage the revolting squadron in the harbor of Rio de Janeiro. Some of the revolting vessels escaped to southern Brazil and the crews of others took refuge on two Portuguese vessels anchored in the harbor.

April 6. The revolt was brought to an end by the sinking of the one remaining vessel in opposition.

November 15. Prudente José de Moraes Barros of São Paulo became the first civilian to assume the Brazilian presidency. Considerable army hostility to him persisted.

1895   February. U.S. President Grover Cleveland handed down an arbitral award in a long-standing Brazilian-Argentine boundary dispute which almost entirely recognized the claims of Brazil.

March. As a measure of discipline the Prudente de Moraes government demoted many of the students in the military academy because of their insubordination.

August 23. Congress voted a general amnesty for the revolutionists of 1893-94.

1896   November. President Prudente de Moraes fell dangerously ill and his duties were assumed by Vice-President Vitorino Pereira. Following divergent policies from those of Moraes, his actions gave rise to great tension between the two on the return of Moraes to the presidency early in 1897.

Initial reverses were suffered by government troops sent to remote Bahia to suppress the activity of a band of religious fanatics led by Antônio Vicente Mendes Maciel, better known as Antônio Conselheiro (the Counselor).

1897   October 5. The Conselheiro stronghold in the interior, Canudos, was taken by storm.

November 5. An unsuccessful attempt to assassinate the

president led to a general revulsion against divisive elements in the politics of Brazil with the result that the last
year of Prudente de Moraes's administration was relatively calm.

1898   June 15. A financial agreement with Great Britain consid-
            erably eased the previously precarious fiscal position of
            Brazil.

            November 15. Another paulista, Manoel Ferras de Campos
            Salles, succeeded to the presidency. Government finances
            continued to improve.

1900   December 1. A long-standing dispute with France over
            the Brazilian-French Guiana boundary was settled favor-
            ably to Brazil.

1901   Brazil successfully settled its controversy with Great Bri-
            tain over its boundary with British Guiana.

1902   November 15. Moraes was succeeded as president by a
            third civilian (and a third paulista), Francisco de Paula
            Rodrigues Alves. Particularly noteworthy in his adminis-
            tration was the work of his minister of public health, Dr.
            Oswaldo Cruz, in improving sanitary conditions and in ex-
            tinguishing or greatly reducing such recurrent hazards as
            those of yellow fever, bubonic plague, and smallpox.

1903   November 17. Settlement of an old boundary controversy
            with Bolivia added about 75,000 square miles to Brazilian
            territory in the west. Credit for this, as well as for nu-
            merous other achievements in foreign affairs, was due to
            the very able foreign minister, Baron Rio Branco, who
            served under four presidents from 1902 to 1912. His vari-
            ous boundary settlements added about 342,000 square miles
            to Brazil's extent.

1904   Brazil and Ecuador settled their boundary controversy.

1905   Brazil negotiated a boundary settlement with Venezuela.

            December 11. The archbishop of Rio de Janeiro became
            Latin America's first Catholic cardinal.

1906   February 26. The Convention of Taubaté, signed by the
            governors of the coffee-producing states of São Paulo,

Minas Gerais, and Rio de Janeiro, introduced the so-
called "valorization" program by which efforts were made
to maintain coffee prices at a profitable level. Coffee production by this time was in serious over-supply and a variety of efforts was made for a long time to maintain prices
and/or reduce production.

July 23. The Third International Conference of American
Republics convened at Rio de Janeiro. It was in session
for about five weeks.

November 15. Affonso Augusto Moreira Penna of Minas
Gerais assumed the presidency. He was especially interested in economic progress for Brazil.

1907   Brazil reached a preliminary settlement of boundary problems with Colombia.

1909   June 14. On the death of President Penna the vice-president,
Nilo Peçanha, assumed the presidency. Peçanha served
for about 17 months. As his successor he threw his influence to the support of Marshal Hermes Rodrigues da Fonseca, nephew of Deodoro da Fonseca, the first president.

September 8. Settlement of a boundary dispute with Peru
added almost 65,000 square miles to Brazil's area.

1910   March 1. The presidential election gave the office to Marshal Hermes da Fonseca. His opponent was Ruy Barbosa.
The campaign was bitterly fought and Hermes's election
marked the climax of a period of growing militarism.

November 15. Marshal Hermes da Fonseca was inaugurated. A full-fledged naval mutiny broke out soon after his
induction and the government had to make important concessions. Hermes's administration was in general inept,
corrupt, and marked by civilian subordination to the military. State governments were overthrown by use of troops
in Bahia, Pernambuco, and two other states.

1914   In the face of serious fiscal problems the government was
forced to issue inconvertible paper money.

August 4. President Hermes declared Brazilian neutrality
at the outbreak of World War I. The war subsequently had
a very grave impact on the Brazilian economy. Both im-

ports and exports fell drastically.

November 15. Wenceslau Braz Pereira Gomes, a civilian from Minas Gerais and vice-president under Hermes, was inaugurated president. He faced all the economic and political problems generated by the war.

1917   April 11. Brazil severed diplomatic relations with the German Empire.

October 26. Brazil declared war on Germany.

1918   November 15. Francisco de Paula Rodrigues Alves was scheduled to assume office at the beginning of a new term but was seriously ill and the vice-president, Delfim Moreira da Costa Ribeiro, had to take over the presidency.

1919   January 18. Rodrigues Alves died, thus necessitating a new election to fill the presidency. The two powerful states of São Paulo and Minas Gerais agreed that the office should go for the remainder of the term to a person from a smaller state, with the tacit assumption that thereafter the two large states would rotate the presidency between them.

July 28. The presidency was occupied by Epitácio Pessôa of Paraíba who at the time was carrying on a very successful work as head of the Brazilian delegation to the Versailles Peace Conference.

1922   June 28. Marshal Hermes da Fonseca violated military discipline by his participation in the presidential campaign and was placed under arrest.

July 5. A revolt by disgruntled elements in the campaign broke out but was quickly suppressed.

September 7. Brazil began an elaborate celebration of the centennial of its independence.

November 15. Artur da Silva Bernardes of Minas Gerais was inaugurated president.

1924   July. Rebellious army elements in São Paulo, an echo of the revolt of 1922, held the city against federal forces for a few weeks.

October. Luiz Carlos Prestes, a former army captain,
led a band of about 1,000 rebels on a long trek through the
interior of Brazil. The march continued for about two
years before the band was overcome by federal troops.
Prestes and other leaders escaped into Bolivia. He later
became Brazil's chief Communist party leader.

1926   Brazil, denied a permanent seat on the Council of the
League of Nations, withdrew from that organization.

In accordance with the tacit agreement between Minas
Gerais and São Paulo there was no real opposition to the
presidential candidacy of a paulista, the state governor,
Washington Luís Pereira de Souza.

November 15. Washington Luís was inaugurated.

1929   The world depression had an immediate effect on Brazil.
Between 1929 and 1931 the price of coffee dropped from
22.5 to 8 cents a pound. Within three years after 1929
Brazil's foreign trade decreased 37 percent by volume and
67 percent by value.

1930   July 25. As the 1930 campaign approached, Washington
Luís, in violation of the unwritten agreement with Minas
Gerais, threw his support for the presidency to the young
paulista governor, Julio Prestes. The governor of Minas
Gerais ahd already promised support for Dr. Getúlio Dor-
nelles Vargas, governor of Rio Grande do Sul. The campaign hence became quite bitter, intensified by Brazil's
economic difficulties. Prestes was declared the winner but
hostility to him and President Washington Luís grew rapidly.

October 3. Revolution broke out in Rio Grande do Sul,
Minas Gerais, and Paraíba. The government was unable
to stop the advance of rebel forces.

October 24. Senior army officers presented Washington
Luís with an ultimatum that he must resign. They then
formed a junta to govern until the situation could be regu-
larized. Washington Luís was held in custody until November 20 when he was permitted to depart for Europe.

October 31. Vargas reached Rio de Janeiro to great ac-
claim. On November 4 he was installed as a provisional
president. He was wiry, realistic, intuitive, pragmatic,
and a political chameleon. He practiced moderation and
affability and eschewed pomp, terror, and inflexibility.
He took energentic steps to try to resolve the economic
crisis, especially as related to coffee marketing.

November 11. Vargas decreed the dissolution of congress
and assumed absolute powers for himself and his government. He appointed interventors to replace the governors
of the states.

1932   February 14. Vargas promulgated a new electoral code
lowering the voting age from 21 to 18, giving the vote to
working women, and guaranteeing a secret ballot; the ban
on voting by illiterates was continued.

June 9. Revolt broke out in the state of São Paulo, which
still felt disgruntlement over the reversal in 1930. The
state put up a strenuous resistance and the revolt continued
for almost three months before federal troops could suppress it. No serious reprisals were taken against the
state, however.

1933   May 3. The president decreed elections for members of
a constituent assembly. This was in part a concession to
São Paulo which had continued to be critical of the new regime.

November. The constituent assembly began its delibera-
tions.

1934   July 16. The new constitution, the republic's second one,
was promulgated and simultaneously Vargas was installed
for a four-year term as constitutional president. The new
basic law continued a federal structure but gave greatly
broadened powers to the national executive. Economic,
social, and cultural provisions of the constitution were
elaborated. The document reflected Italian corporative
influences.

1935   November 25. Revolt, allegedly leftist inspired, broke
out it Natal, capital of Rio Grande do Norte. It was quickly suppressed but martial law remained in effect for more
than a year and thousands of arrests were made.

1937   As elections scheduled for January, 1938 approached the
              political fever of the country increased markedly. Var-
              gas's opportunistic course was threatened by Communist
              opposition from the left and that of the Integralists, a na-
              tionalistic and confused but large group, from the right.
              Three presidential candidates emerged; Vargas was con-
              stitutionally ineligible to succeed himself.

              November 10. Vargas engineered a coup d'etat by which
              he assumed dictatorial power, supplanted the 1934 consti-
              tution with a new one of his own drafting, dissolved con-
              gress, deposed most of the state governors, and thus in-
              augurated "the new state." The new constitution (never
              formally promulgated) vastly increased the president's
              powers and decreased those of the states. Complicated
              legislative machinery was provided but never implemented.
              For more than seven years Vargas ruled by decree.

1938   May 10. Integralists mounted a spectacular attack on the
              presidental palace, fought off for some hours by Vargas,
              his daughter, and staff, until loyal supporting troops ar-
              rived.

              By 1938 Germany had gained dramatically in trade with Bra-
              zil and actually slightly exceeded the United States as a
              supplier of Brazilian imports.

1939   Brazil remained officially neutral in World War II although
              popular sentiment was strongly sympathetic with the Allied
              cause.

1942   January 15. The Third Foreign Ministers' Conference,
              meeting as a consequence of the Japanese attack at Pearl
              Harbor in December, 1941, convened at Rio de Janeiro.

              January 28. Brazil, along with all other Western Hemi-
              sphere states except Argentina and Chile, which had not
              already declared war on Nazi Germany, broke diplomatic
              relations with the Axis powers.

              August. German submarines within three days in mid-
              August sank five Brazilian ships with a considerable loss
              of life. Brazil responded with a declaration of war on Ger-
              many and Italy on August 22. Establishment of U.S. air
              and naval bases on the Brazilian "hump" was authorized,
              the Brazilian navy was active in patrolling the south Atlan-

tic, and in 1944 an expeditionary force of 25,000 troops was sent to take part in the Italian campaign.

1944   Slowly building pressures brought Vargas late in the year to take halting steps to return Brazil to democratic rule. He relaxed censorship and cautiously permitted renewed political activity.

1945   February. The government decreed a law to regulate voter registration and election of a president. Vargas set December 1945 as the date for presidential and congressional elections.

February. July. Sentiment, which many felt to be manipulated, began to crystallize around the queremistas, i.e., those who wanted Vargas to remain in power.

October 10. Vargas suddenly moved up the date for all state and local elections to December 2.

October 25. Vargas further stimulated speculation about his intentions by appointing his brother Benjamin as chief of police of Rio de Janeiro. The feeling became widespread that he was preparing a further coup, as in 1937.

October 29. The military high command undertook its own coup and forced the resignation of Vargas, who retired to his estate in Rio Grande do Sul. The military named José Linhares, chief justice of the supreme court, as provisional president until after the elections, which were left for the date set.

December 2. Three recently formed major parties (and several smaller ones) participated in the elections. Vargas had inspired two of them, the Social Democratic party, chiefly rural and based on various state political machines, and the Brazilian Labor party, initially the personal political machine of Vargas himself. The third was the National Democratic Union, including chiefly those who opposed Vargas. The winner was Gen. Eurico Gaspar Dutra, Vargas's war minister and the candidate of the Social Democrats. The elections also demonstrated Vargas's continued popularity with many people: he was elected a senator from two states and a deputy from six and the federal district (and of course had to choose one seat from those to which he was elected).

1946   January 31. Gen. Dutra was inaugurated president. He
                        was taciturn and colorless and, as a politician, awkward.

                        September 18. A new constitution, drafted by the congress
                        elected in December, 1945 was promulgated. It maintained
                        the Vargas labor legislation but attempted to limit presi-
                        tial authoritarianism.

                        A large steel plant at Volta Redonda, between Rio de Jan-
                        eiro and São Paulo, went into operation.   /

1947   January. The Communists made startling gains in state
                        elections. Later in the year the electoral court declared
                        the party illegal and it went underground, but just barely.

1950   The presidential campaign was largely lackluster except
                        for the race of Getúlio Vargas for a new presidential
                        term. Vargas was nominally the candidate of the Labor
                        party but in reality his campaign was based on personal
                        popularity. He won overwhelmingly.

1951   January 31. Vargas was inaugurated as president, the
                        first time he had filled the office by popular election.
                        His political magic was now largely gone, however, and
                        his term was anticlimactic.

1953   October. The Brazilian Petroleum Corporation (Petrobras)
                        was established by law and given a monopoly over exploi-
                        tation of petroleum.

1954   Dissatisfaction with the Vargas regime, especially with
                        his labor minister, João Goulart, mounted. Early in the
                        year 82 colonels presented a demand that Goulart and the
                        war minister must be dismissed. Vargas gave in to the
                        pressure and removed both.

                        August 5. Carlos Lacerda, an influential newspaper edi-
                        tor highly critical of the Vargas government, was attacked
                        by would-be assassins. He was only slightly wounded but
                        an air force major accompanying him was killed. Investi-
                        gation quickly involved the president's personal guard in
                        responsibility for the attack. The popular uproar was
                        tremendous.

                        August 24. The military presented Vargas with an ultima-
                        tum that he must resign. Vargas retired to his rooms and

soon thereafter shot and killed himself. He left a cryptic and emotional letter suggesting that "international groups" had been responsible for his downfall and death. He was succeeded by Vice-President João Café Filho (the "Filho" means Junior). Politicking for the 1955 presidential election began quickly.

1955   October. Juscelino Kubitschek, governor of Minas Gerais, was elected president and Goulart vice-president. Illness of Café and military suspicion that an effort might be made to prevent inauguration of the newly elected officials brought two changes in the presidency in the next few weeks.

1956   January 31. Kubitschek and Goulart were inaugurated. The president used the slogan "fifty years' progress in five" and set as a special goal the construction of the long-planned national capital in the interior of the country. He also emphasized road building and during his five-year term opened some 11,000 miles of new roads.

1958   Nationalistic criticism of the United States increased rapidly.

1960   April 21. The spectacular new capital, Brasília, in the inland state of Goias, was inaugurated with elaborate ceremony. Its cost had been an estimated $700 million. The former federal district including Rio de Janeiro was converted into the new state of Guanabara, Brazil's smallest state in area.

October. The elections placed Jânio da Silva Quadros, candidate of the National Democratic Union and former governor of São Paulo, in the top office and Goulart again in the vice-presidency. Quadros's campaign was largely personalistic and he pledged to eliminate inefficiency and corruption in government.

1961   January 31. Quadros and Goulart were inaugurated.

April 16. Quadros and Carlos Lacerda, now governor of Guanabara, came to a political parting of the ways over Brazilian policy toward the United States and Cuba. Friction between the president and congress thereafter deepened rapidly.

August 19. Granting by Quadros of a high Brazilian award to Che Guevera, the Cuban revolutionary leader, brought violent new protests from Lacerda. On August 23 and 24 Lacerda made television charges that Quadros was planning a coup involving dismissal of congress.

August 25. Quadros abruptly resigned and departed from Brasília. He apparently hoped his resignation would be refused and his powers increased but congress quickly accepted the resignation. Vice-president Goulart at the time was in China on a trade mission and doubt persisted for a time as to whether the military would accept him as president. Congress promptly adopted constitutional amendments effecting a parliamentary form of government in which the cabinet members would be responsible to congress.

September 7. On the basis of the compromise over the executive power Goulart assumed the presidency. He had only limited authority but exercised that power freely. He promptly displayed a friendly policy toward the Castro regime in Cuba and toward various Communist countries. His domestic policies were erratic and opportunistic.

1962   September 3. Goulart approved a law limiting profit remittances abroad. This soon resulted in a drastic decrease in foreign investments in Brazil. At the same time inflation was increasing rapidly. The parliamentary system seemed unable to cope with the serious economic problems.

1963   January 6. In a plebiscitary vote which congress had authorized, the Brazilians by an overwhelming majority approved a return to presidential government. Congress promptly acquiesced in the necessary changes but did not become basically more cooperative with Goulart.

March. Congress turned down an agrarian reform bill urged by Goulart. The president's policies veered increasingly toward the left.

1964   March 13. An emotional political rally in Rio de Janeiro seemed to confirm the demagogic course of Goulart.

March 25. A mass meeting of enlisted sailors and marines shouted approval of Goulart's actions.

March 30. Goulart made an inflammatory television address highly critical of the army officer class. By this time Brazil's fiscal position was approaching the chaotic.

March 31. Army units marched on Rio de Janeiro from Minas Gerais. The whole situation immediately disintegrated. A military coup deposed Goulart who the following day flew to Brasília and then to southern Brazil but was unable to rally support.

April 4. Goulart went into exile in Uruguay. In the meantime the head of the chamber of deputies had declared the presidency vacant and had himself assumed the acting presidency.

April 9. The supreme military command issued the "First Institutional Act, " enlarging the powers of the presidency and calling on congress to elect a president. Military leaders selected Gen. Humberto de Alencar Castelo Branco for the presidency, though the choice was nominally made by congress.

April 11. Castelo Branco assumed the presidency. Although he seemed personally moderate the new military regime drastically purged Brazilian political life, depriving some 400 prominent persons of their political rights for 10 years. Subordinate military officers acted very heavy-handedly.

1965   Castelo Branco's term, originally designed to extend to January 31, 1966, was subsequently extended to March 15, 1967. He followed generally conservative economic policies, although financial concessions to military officers were excessive. As time passed the government's repressive activities became more extreme.

Elections in October revealed that despite close governmental controls the popularity of the military regime was waning.

October 27. The Second Institutional Act liquidated all old political parties and established two synthetic new parties, one pro-government and one ostensibly anti-government.

1966   February 5. The Third Institutional Act ended popular election of state and local officials and substituted indirect election or appointment.

October 3. The complaisant congress elected the military choice, Gen. Artur da Costa e Silva, to succeed Castelo Branco as president the following year.

December. An extremely severe censorship measure was decreed.

1967   March 15. General Costa e Silva assumed the presidency. He seemed less aloof than his predecessor and appeared interested in industrialization and economic development. He was under strong pressures from both right and left and became increasingly indecisive. Both the supreme court and congress began showing a few signs of independence of military domination.

1968   December 13. The Fifth Institutional Act disbanded congress and the state legislatures, suspended the constitution, imposed new censorship, and gave the president dictatorial powers.

1969   January. Resignation of the minister of the interior, who had favored agrarian reform and social welfare legislation, confirmed the ascendancy of the hard-line military wing.

August 30. President Costa e Silva suffered a stroke, which necessitated his replacement. Instead of allowing the civilian vice-president to take his place the military leaders constituted themselves as an extra-legal junta for a short time.

September 4. Urban guerrillas kidnapped the U.S. ambassador to Brazil and as conditions for his safe release demanded that the radio, television, and newspapers must publicize a guerrilla anti-government statement and that 15 political prisoners must be flown to asylum in Mexico. The government complied and the ambassador was released on September 7.

October 7. The junta named Gen. Emílio Garrastazú Médici as president.

October 22. The junta reconvened a thoroughly chastened congress.

October 30. General Médici assumed office for a term to
end March 15, 1974. The government promulgated a new
constitution drafted by Costa e Silva, and only slightly
changed later, which further weakened congress.

1971   Repression by the military regime continued unabated and
            was alleviated only by gradually improving economic con-
            ditions.

            January 16. The Swiss ambassador, who had been kidnapped
            40 days earlier, was released after 70 political prisoners
            had been given Chilean asylum.

            February 18. A Brazilian bishops' conference supported
            two bishops who had protested government torture of poli-
            tical prisoners.

            July 6. President Médici decreed an agrarian reform law
            for the Northeast.

1972   November 15. The government, with about 70 per cent of
            the vote, won municipal elections.

1973   January 2. A report by the Inter-American Press Associ-
            ation claimed that Brazil had no press freedom whatever.

            Reports circulated that Patiño tin interests, formerly
            dominant in mining in Bolivia, might become involved in
            possible exploitation of Brazil's allegedly considerable
            tin resources.

            March 17. The Brazilian National Council of Bishops de-
            nounced governmental repression and discrimination a-
            gainst peasants, workers, blacks, women, and others.

            April 28. The Rio de Janeiro weekly Manchete, often con-
            sidered a government mouthpiece, predicted that Brazil
            would adopt a "great-power" policy and would considerably
            increase military aviation equipment and other armaments.

            June 18. President Médici announced that he would be suc-
            ceeded on March 15, 1974, by retired General Ernesto
            Geisel, president of the government petroleum producing
            monopoly, Petrobras. The election would ostensibly be in
            the hands of an electoral college but, assuming the contin-
            uance of military domination, the result would be a fore-
            gone conclusion.

DOCUMENTS

THE TREATY OF TORDESILLAS (1494)

The premature decision by the Pope in 1493 dividing new lands to be discovered between the Spanish and the Portuguese was unsatisfactory to the latter and the following year the Portuguese King João was able to obtain a reconsideration of the boundary from the Spanish. The change was negotiated at a small town in northern Spain and was embodied in the Treaty of Tordesillas, June 7, 1494. The treaty provision that the new dividing line should be surveyed within ten months was never carried out. This gave some semblance of excuse to the restless paulistas later to explore and settle far to the west of where Portuguese territory presumably ended. Given the independent nature of the roving bandeirantes, however, they probably would have been little bound by the limitations of such an international agreement under any circumstances.

The relevant portions of the Treaty of Tordesillas are in the following excerpt.

Thereupon it was declared by the above-mentioned representatives of the aforesaid King and Queen (Ferdinand and Isabella) of Castile, Léon, Aragon, Sicily, Granada, etc., and of the aforesaid King (João) of Portugal and the Algarves, etc.:

1. That, whereas a certain controversy exists between the said lords, their constituents, as to what lands, of all those discovered in the ocean sea up to the present day, the date of this treaty, pertain to each one of the said parts respectively; therefore, for the sake of peace and concord, and for the preservation of the relationship and love of the said King of Portugal for the said King and Queen of Castile, Aragon, etc., it being the pleasure of their Highnesses, they, their said representatives, acting in their name and by virtue of their powers herein described, covenanted and agreed that a boundary or straight line be determined and drawn north and south, from pole to pole, on the said ocean sea, from the Arctic to the Antarctic pole. This boundary or line shall be drawn straight, as aforesaid, at a distance of three hundred and seventy leagues west of the Cape Verde Islands, being calculated by degrees, or by any other manner as may be considered the best and readiest, provided the distance shall be no greater than abovesaid. And all lands, both islands and mainlands, found and discovered already, or to be found and discovered hereafter, by the said King of Portugal and by his vessels on this side of the said line and bound determined as above, toward the east, in either north or south latitude, on the eastern side of the said bound, provided the said bound is not crossed, shall belong to, and remain in the possession of, and pertain forever to, the said King of Portugal and his successors. And all other lands, both islands and mainlands, found or to be found hereafter, discovered or to be discovered hereafter, which have been discovered or shall be discovered by the said King and Queen

of Castile, Aragon, etc., and by their vessels, on the western side of
said bound, determined as above, after having passed the said bound toward the west, in either its north or south latitude, shall belong to, and
remain in the possession of, and pertain forever to, the said King and
Queen of Castile, Léon, etc., and to their successors.

2. Item, the said representatives promise and affirm by virtue of
the powers aforesaid, that from this date no ships shall be despatched --
namely as follows: the said King and Queen of Castile, Léon, Aragon,
etc., for this part of the bound, and its eastern side, on this side of the
said bound, which pertains to the said King of Portugal and the Algarves,
etc.; nor the said King of Portugal to the other part of the said bound
which pertains to the said King and Queen of Castile, Aragon, etc. -- for
the purpose of discovering and seeking any mainlands or islands, or for
the purpose of trade, barter, or conquest of any kind. But should it come
to pass that the said ships of the said King and Queen of Castile, Léon,
Aragon, etc., on sailing thus on this side of the said bound, should discover any mainlands or islands in the region pertaining, as abovesaid,
to the said King of Portugal, such mainlands or islands shall pertain to
and belong forever to the said King of Portugal and his heirs, and their
Highnesses shall order them to be surrendered to him immediately. And
if the said ships of the said King of Portugal discover any islands and
mainlands in the regions of the said King and Queen of Castile, Léon,
Aragon, etc., all such lands shall belong to and remain forever in the
possession of the said King and Queen of Castile, Léon, Aragon, etc.,
and their heirs, and the said King of Portugal shall cause such lands to
be surrendered immediately.

3. Item, in order that the said line or bound may be made straight
and as nearly as possible the said distance of three hundred and seventy
leagues west of the Cape Verde Islands, as hereinbefore stated, the said
representatives of both the said parties agree and assent that within the
ten months immediately following the date of this treaty their said constituent lords shall despatch two or four caravels, namely, one or two by
each of them, a greater or less number, as they may mutually consider
necessary. These vessels shall meet at the Grand Canary Island during
this time, and each one of the said parties shall send certain persons in
them, to wit, pilots, astrologers, sailors, and any others they may deem
desirable. But there must be as many on one side as on the other, and
certain of the said pilots, astrologers, sailors, and others of those sent
by the said King and Queen of Castile, Aragon, etc., and who are experienced, shall embark in the ships of the said King of Portugal and the
Algarves; in like manner certain of the said persons sent by the King
of Portugal shall embark in the ship or ships of the said King and Queen
of Castile, Aragon, etc.; a like number in each case, so that they may
jointly study and examine to better advantage the sea, courses, winds,
and the degree of the sun or of north latitude, and lay out the leagues
aforesaid, in order that, in determining the line and boundary, all sent
and empowered by both the said parties in the said vessels, shall jointly
concur. These said vessels shall continue their course together to the
Cape Verde Islands, from whence they shall lay a direct course to the
west, to the distance of the said three hundred and seventy degrees,

measured as the said persons shall agree, and measured without prejudice to the said parties. When this point is reached, such point will constitute the place and mark for measuring degrees of the sun or of north latitude either by daily runs measured in leagues, or in any other manner that shall mutually be deemed better. This said line shall be drawn north and south as aforesaid, from the said Arctic pole to the said Antarctic pole. And when this line has been determined as abovesaid, those sent by each of the aforesaid parties, to whom each one of the said parties must delegate his own authority and power, to determine the said mark and bound, shall draw up a writing concerning it and affix thereto their signatures. And when determined by the mutual consent of all of them, this line shall be considered as a perpetual mark and bound, in such wise that the said parties, or either of them, or their future successors, shall be unable to deny it, or erase or remove it, at any time or in any manner whatsoever. And should, perchance, the said line and bound from pole to pole, as aforesaid, intersect any island or mainland, at the first point of such intersection of such island or mainland by the said line, some kind of mark or tower shall be erected, and a succession of similar marks shall be erected in a straight line from such mark or tower, in a line identical with the above-mentioned bound. These marks shall separate those portions of such land belonging to each one of the said parties; and the subjects of the said parties shall not dare, on either side, to enter the territory of the other, by crossing the said mark or bound in such island or mainland.

4. Item, inasmuch as the said ships of the said King and Queen of Castile, Léon, Aragon, etc., sailing as before declared, from their kingdoms and seignories to their said possessions on the other side of the said line, must cross the seas on this side of the line, pertaining to the said King of Portugal, it is therefore concerted and agreed that the said ships of the said King and Queen of Castile, Léon, Aragon, etc., shall, at any time and without any hindrance, sail in either direction, freely, securely, and peacefully, over the said seas of the said King of Portugal, and within the said line. And whenever their Highnesses and their successors wish to do so, and deem it expedient, their said ships may take their courses and routes direct from their kingdoms to any region within their line and bound to which they desire to despatch expeditions of discovery, conquest, and trade. They shall take their courses direct to the desired region and for any purpose desired therein, and shall not leave their course, unless compelled to do so by contrary weather. They shall do this provided that, before crossing the said line, they shall not seize or take possession of anything discovered in his said region by the said King of Portugal; and should their said ships find anything before crossing the said line, as aforesaid, it shall belong to the said King of Portugal, and their Highnesses shall order it surrendered immediately. ...

EARLY ENGLISH TRADE (1540)

Unlike the French and the Dutch, the English were more interested in Brazilian trade than in occupation or colonization.
At first, the attraction of brazilwood was a magnet for them as
it was for the other two European countries. The following account, not always easy to read because of its archaic spelling,
is taken from the "Voyage of the Barbara to Brazil, Anno 1540,"
edited by R. G. Marsden in Sir John K. Laughton (ed.), The Naval
Miscellany, Publications of the Navy Records Society, v. 2 (London: Navy Records Society, 1912).

On Phelippe and Jacobbes day in the mornyng we fell with an ilande
in the see, and there wente on lande with our boate and found nother man
nor childe, but only fowle and bestes and cotten and peper there growyng.
And there we dyd tary all day, and that nyght wente on borde withe our
boate, and so ymmediatly departed and sayled from thens unto the lande
of Brasell, and fell with the land in iiij [four] dayes after ensueng. This
don we ankered, and our pilot withe our specheman went on lande to
here news, and ymmediatly came on borde agayne and toulde us. Here
is no brasell to get, for we be fallen xlty [forty] leages to lye warde
[leeward] of that place where the brasell dothe growe, for the people
sayde that they wolde not brynge it so farre unto us. Then, this saying,
they sayde ther was no remedy but that we muste nedes go thither withe
oure shyp. And as we were turnyng thothurwarde [southward], we stake
on the rockes with the shyppe, and like to have loste her clene, so that
we had her of agayne, and she was sore leake, and the pilotte then sayde
that it was not possible to turne thether with our shyppe, the way was
so dangerous, wherfore our shyppe shall remain still here, and we will
sende furthe oure greate boate and barcke and put our wares in them,
they do drawe but lytle water and be nymble and therfore they be neces-
sarieste for to goe and come to fetche our ladyng hether. This doon they
departed frome us and was frome us xij [twelve] dayes yende they returned to us agayne, and were in greate jeopardy of losyng bothe boote
and barcke. And the people of the countrey toulde us that it was not possible to have no brasell there, for because we were so farre shotte to
lyewarde of it. And then oure pilotte dyd say, to tarry here and to spende
our vyctuall it is but folly and have no proffet; for here is a place to
lyewards of us which is called Callybalde, which I know very well, and
it is C leages hense, and thethur I will, and there we shall have oure
ladyng of cotten and beastes in a shorte space. And therethur we came
and there ankoryed, and our pilotte with our specheman [interpreter]
wente on shore, and dyd speak withe the people; and so doon they dyd
come on borde us, and they sayde they wer glad of our comyng and prom-
esed us to have of ther commodyties for our wares gladly, as our specheman tolde us. This doon our master commaunded us withe the captayne
and pilotte to goe ashore and there to build an house; and at ther com-

maundment we so dyd, and caryed wares on lande, and dyd bye and sell with them for cotten; and there we were for the space of xijth dayes, and bought certen cottens in them for our wares. And there came to us a Portyugale and a Frencheman and certen of the same countrey with them by lande, and asked of us whence we were, and we sayd of Englande, and he demaunded us wherfore we dyd enterprise to come there. We answered we came for the trade of merchaundyse as they and other doe with us, etc. And then he commaunded us in his kynges name for to avoyde the countrey, and not to tary therein upon payne of a further dysplesure to us hereafter ensueing. Then we made hym answer that we wolde not departe for hym for thuttermoste that he could do in any weys to us. And upon the sayd answer he departed in a greate fury, and sayd he wolde make us repente the tyme that ever we dyd enterprise so boldeley and wolde not avoyde at this commaundemente, and so wente his wey. And we contynued in our trade with the people of the countrey still. So that the nexte night after foloweng, aboute xij of the clocke at nyght, the same Frencheman whiche was with the Portyugale before, and a man of the same countrey, whiche the Portyugale dyd sende with hym alongeste on the water to our shyppe for thentente that they wolde have cut our cable that our shyppe shulde have dreven on the rockes. And we beyng on watche, parceavyng thentente of the sayde Frencheman and thother, dyd take them and kepte them till the nexte day in the mornyng, and our captayne dyd demaunde wherfore that they dyd come, and they sayd that they came to by part of our wares; and then we tolde the Frencheman that we wolde ponysshe hym onlesse that he wolde shewe us the truythe wher fore he dyd come. And he sayd that in case he wolde not dooe me no hurte, I wolde tell you the truthe of oure purpose for comyng hether. Oure Captayne answeryed and sayd he wolde not. And then he dyd confesse the truythe as is before rehersyd, that it was to cut our cable, etc. And then we kepte hym with us iiij dayes, and at the iiij days end we dyd carry hym on lande to helpe us to doe our besynes. And in suche tyme as we wer moste besyeste aboute our cheffe besynes he dyd scape away frome us. Then the thrydde nyght after that he was thus goon our spechemen and xijth moe of the Frenchemen of our company which did use to lye on shore in oure house to make our marketts withe the people of that countrey dyd ron away in that sayd nyght and caryed withe them all the wares whiche were on lande in our bowthe [booth] withe them clene, and had withe them an English man, which was our cockswayne. And in the mornyng our boate came on lande so sone as we could se; and then ij of our company beyng Englysshe men whiche wer smethes and lay on lande in a forge that they wroguth on be sydes our bowthe, dyd shewe us that oure Frenchemen wer goon away in the nyght, and lefte nothing in ther bowthe. And this we herying John Podde and fyvetene other of our company folowed them, and made greate spede after to fetche them agayne. And then when they wer lj leages above in the wodds they besett our company with people of the countrey, and so in conclusion set uppon them, and dyd slay them all save one man by the councell of the Frencheman and the Portyugale, and that tyme we were at the water side besye within our bowthe. And the same after none there came above a mll of the people and sette oure bowthe on fyer, we beyng within; in so moche as then they burned all our cotten that we had brought that we saved not a dell [fraction, or small part] of it. Then we fought with them iiij houres by the clocke, and in conclusion we beate them of, but dyvers of our men were hurte. And at the laste we gote oure boate and wente on borde of oure owne shyppe, and rode there till the nexte day in the mornyng. And then we sent our boate on shore and caused a banner of truse to be set up to them, and withe it a sworde and hatchett, and withe it a letter wherein was written to the Frenchmen, yf they had any of our men that wer a lyfe, to sende them to us, and we wolde geve them ther owne asking for them. This doon the people of the countrey returned agaynste us agayne, and a great nomber of them, and dyd shote at us, and beate us of the lande, and wolde not suffer us to lande ther no more. And at that tyme we toke iij of them and brought them on borde with us, and there we dyd that daye, and coulde not be suffered to come on lande; in so moche that then oure captayne and our other officers sayde, Masters ye se that we cannot be sufferyd to doe our besynes as touchyng our purpose, wherfore it shalbe moste meatiste for us to get homewarde, for here we doe but lose tyme, and our victualls are almost goon.

·   ·   ·   ·   ·   ·   ·

THE MIGHTY AMAZON (1639)

The mighty Amazon, the world's greatest river in volume, was discovered early. It was Vicente Yáñez Pinzón, commanding a Spanish expedition, who first found it, in 1500. He ascended the river for some fifty miles from the Atlantic. It was again "discovered," and first descended, by Francisco de Orellana who, going down from the towering Andes by way of the Napo River, explored the full length of the Amazon in his famous voyage in 1539-41. Twenty years later the Spanish adventurer Lope de Aguirre led his plundering expedition down the river. But no Inca gold was to be found in the land of the fabled Amazons, no great civilizations, even, so they thought at first, no natural resources of value. A small Spanish expedition down river in 1636 stimulated a major Portuguese exploring venture up the Amazon. A large expedition was dispatched by canoe upstream and ultimately reached Quito. It returned to the Atlantic in 1639 after two years of the most thorough exploration the Amazon had yet received.

On the return voyage a Spanish priest, Cristóval de Acuña, accompanied the Portuguese party and subsequently wrote A New Discovery of the Great River of the Amazons, from which the following excerpts are taken. Acuña's account was published in Clements R. Markham (ed.), Expeditions into the Valley of the Amazons (London: Hakluyt Society, 1859).

THE VOYAGE

On the 16th February 1639, they commenced their long voyage (downstream), which lasted for a space of ten months, when they entered the city of Pará, on the 12th of December of the same year. After they had crossed those lofty mountains on foot, which, with the liquor of their veins, feed and sustain that great river; they voyaged on the waves to where, spread out into eighty-four mouths, it pays its mighty tribute to the sea. They, with particular care, took notes of all that was worthy of remark, measured the heights, noted down all the tributary rivers by their names, became acquainted with the nations who dwell on their banks, beheld their fertility, enjoyed the resources of the great river, experienced its climate, and finally left nothing of which they could not say that they had been eye-witnesses. As such, as persons whom so many considerations oblige to be accurate, I pray to those who read this narrative that they will give me the credit that is just, for I am one of those, and in the name of both I took up my pen to write. I say this because other accounts may be brought to light, which will not be so truthful as this narrative. This will be a true account, and it is an account of things which, with face uncovered, not more than fifty Spaniards and Portuguese can testify to, namely, those who made the same voyage. I affirm that which is certain as certain, and that which is doubtful as such, that in an affair of so much importance, no one may believe more than is stated in this narrative.

The River of Amazons is the Largest in the World

The famous river of Amazons, which traverses the richest, most fertile, and most densely populated regions of Peru, may be, from this day forth, proclaimed as the largest and most celebrated river in the whole world. For if the Ganges irrigates all India, and, with the great volume of its waters, eclipses the sea itself, which loses its very name and is called the Gangetic Gulf (or sometimes the Bay of Bengal): if the Euphrates, the famed river of Syria and Persia, is the joy and delight of those countries: if the Nile irrigates and fertilizes a great part of Africa: the river of Amazons waters more extensive regions, fertilizes more plains, supports more people, and augments by its floods a mightier ocean: it only wants, in order to surpass them in felicity, that its source should be in Paradise; as is affirmed of those other rivers, by grave authors.

The narrowest part in which the river collects its waters, is little more than a quarter of a league wide. A place, doubtless, which has been provided by divine Providence, where the great sea of fresh water narrows itself, so that a fortress may be built to impede the passage of any hostile armament of what force soever; in case it should enter by the principal mouth of this mighty river.

The depth of the river is great, and there are parts where no bottom has yet been found. From the mouth to the Rio Negro, a distance of nearly six hundred leagues, there is never less than thirty or forty brazas [fathoms] in the main channel; above the Rio Negro it varies more, from twenty to twelve or eight brazas, but up to very near its source there is sufficient depth for any vessel; and, though the current would impede the ascent, yet there is not wanting usually, every day, three or four hours of strong breeze, which would assist in overcoming it.

Islands, Their Fertility and Products

All this river is full of islands, some large, others small, and so numerous that it is impossible to count them, for they are met with at every turn. Some are four or five leagues, others ten, others twenty in circumference, and that which is inhabited by the Tupinambas (of whom I shall speak hereafter), is more than a hundred leagues round.

There are also many other very small ones, on which the Indians sow their seeds, having their habitations on the larger ones. These islands are flooded by the river every year, and are so fertilized by the mud which it leaves behind, that they can never be called sterile. The ordinary products, which are maize and yuca, or manioc, the commonest food of all, are in great abundance; and though it would seem that the Indians are exposed to great loss, on account of the powerful floods; yet nature, the common mother of us all, has provided these barbarians with an easy means of preserving their food. They collect the yucas, which are roots from which they make the casava, the ordinary substitute for bread in all parts of Brazil; and forming caves or deep holes in the earth, they bury them, and leave them well covered up during all the time of the floods. When the waters subside, they take them out, and use them for food, without their having lost any part of their virtue. If nature teaches the ant to store up grain in the bowels of the earth, to serve for food during a whole year: how much more will she suggest a contrivance to the Indian, how barbarous soever he may be, to protect him from harm, and to preserve his food: for is it not certain that Divine Providence will take more care of men than of dumb animals?

The Kinds of Liquor Which They Use

This [yuca?] is, as I have said, the daily bread which always accompanied their other food; and it not only serves for food, but also as a drink, to which all the natives are usually much inclined. For this purpose they make large thin cakes, which they place in an oven and bake, so that they will last for many months: these they keep in the highest part of their houses, to preserve them from the dampness of the earth. When they wish to use them, they melt them in water, and having boiled the liquor at a fire, they let it stand as long as is necessary; and, when cold, it is the usual wine which they drink. It is sometimes so strong that it might be taken for grape wine, and intoxicates the natives, making them lose their judgment.

With the help of this wine they celebrate their feasts, mourn their dead, receive their visitors, sow and reap their crops; indeed there is no occasion on which they meet, that this liquor is not the mercury which attracts them and the riband which detains them. They also make, though they are not so common, other kinds of wine, of the wild fruits which abound on the trees, so fond are they of drunkenness. They put the juice into water, and produce a liquor which often exceeds beer in strength, that beverage which is so much used in foreign countries. These wines are kept in large earthen jars, like those used in Spain; also in small pipes made of one piece of the hollowed trunk of a tree; and in large vases woven from herbs, and so smeared with bitumen, that not one drop of the liquor which they contain is ever lost.

The Fruits Which They Have

The food with which they accompany their bread and wine is of various kinds -- not only fruits, such as plantains, pine apples, and guavas, but very palatable chestnuts, which in Peru they call "almonds of the Sierra," for in truth they more resemble the latter than the former. They name them chestnuts, because they are enclosed in shells which resemble the prickly husk of the real chestnut. The Indians also have palms of different kinds, some of which produce cocoa nuts, others palatable dates which, though wild, are of a very pleasant taste. There are also many other different kinds of fruits, all proper to tropical climates. They have likewise nourishing roots such as the potatoe, the yuca mansas, which the Portuguese call macachera, garas, criadillas de terra, and others which, either roasted or boiled, are not only palatable, but also very nutritious.

Nature of the Land, and of Medicinal Drugs

From this mildness of the climate arises without doubt the freshness of all the banks of this river, which, crowned with various beautiful trees, appear to be continually delineating new countries, in which nature brightens, and art is taught. Although for the most part the land is low, it also has tolerably high rising grounds, small plains clear of trees and covered with flowers, valleys which always retain moisture, and, in more distant parts, hills which may properly receive the name of Cordilleras.

In the wild forests the natives have, for their sicknesses, the best dispensary of medicines; for they collect the largest cañafistula, or fruit of the purging cassia, that has even been found; the best sarsaparilla; healing gums and resins in great abundance: and honey of wild bees at every step, so abundant that there is scarcely a place where it is not found, and it is not only useful medicinally, but also very pleasant and palatable as food. The wax, though black, is good, and burns as well as any other.

In these forests too are the oil of andirova, trees of priceless value for curing wounds; here too is the copaiba, which has no equal as a balsam; here too are found a thousand kinds of herbs and trees of very peculiar qualities; and to find many others a second Dioscorides or a third Pliny should come out, to investigate their properties.

Timber and Materials for Ships

The woods of this river are innumerable, so tall that they reach to the clouds, so thick that it causes astonishment. I measured a cedar with my hands, which was thirty palmas in circumference. They are nearly all of such good wood that better could not be desired; there are cedars, cotton trees, iron wood trees, and many others now made known in those parts, and proved to be the best in the world for building vessels. In this river vessels may be built better and at less cost than in any other country, finished and launched, without the necessity of sending anything from Europe, except iron for the nails. Here, as I have said, is timber; here are cables made from the bark of a certain tree, which will hold a ship in the heaviest gale; here is excellent pitch and tar; here is oil, as well vegetable as from fish; here they can make excellent oakum which they call embira, for caulking the ships, and also there is nothing better for the string of an arquebuss; here is cotton for the sails; and here finally is a great multitude of people, so that there is nothing wanting, for building as many vessels as may be placed on the stocks.

Of Four Valuable Products Found on the Banks of This River

There are on the banks of the great river of the Amazons four products, which, if cultivated, would undoubtedly be sufficient to enrich not only one, but many kingdoms. The first of these is the timber; of which, besides there being so many curious kinds, of great value; there are such quantities fit for building that while as much may be cut as is wanted, there will be the certainty that the supply can never be exhausted.

The second kind is the cocoa, of which the banks of this river are so full that in some places the wood of it would suffice, if cut, for lodging a whole army. There is scarcely any difference between this tree, and that which yields this much valued fruit in New Spain; which, when cultivated, is of such value that the trees, growing a foot apart, are every year worth eight silver rials, after all expenses are paid. It is clear with what little labour these trees may be cultivated on this river, when, without any help from art, nature alone covers them with abundance of fruit.

The third kind is tobacco, of which great quantities are found, in all the country near the banks of this river, and if it were cultivated with the care that this seed requires, it would be the best in the world. In the opinion of those who understand the subject, the soil and climate are all that can be desired to produce prolific harvests.

The product which, in my view, ought to be most cultivated on this river is sugar, which is the fourth kind. It is the most noble, most productive, most certain, and most valuable to the royal crown; and many farms ought to be established, which in a short time would restore the losses on the Brazilian coast. For this purpose neither much time nor much labour would be necessary, nor what now-a-days is more dreaded, much outlay, for the land for sugar cane is the most productive in all Brazil, as we can testify who have visited those parts; and the floods, which never last more than a few days, leave it so fertile that it might be thought to be too rich. Nor will it be a new thing to raise sugar cane on the banks of this river; for along its whole vast length, from its first sources, we were always meeting with it: so that it seemed from that time to give signs of its future increase, when mills should be established to work it. These would not be expensive, because all necessary timber is at hand, with water in abundance. Copper is alone wanting, which with great ease might be supplied from Spain, in anticipation of the rich return which would be afterwards received.

Of Other Valuable Products

Not only may these four products be promised, from this newly discovered land, to supply the whole world; but there are also many others, which, though in less quantities, would not fail to enrich the royal crown. Such, among others, is the cotton which is picked in abundance; the uruca, which gives the best dye, and is much valued by foreigners; the fruit of the cassia; the sarsaparilla; the oils which rival the best balsams in curing wounds; the gums and sweet resins; the agave, whence the best cord is obtained, which is plentiful, and many others; which necessity, or the desire of riches, are bringing to light every day.

THE INDIANS

All this new world, if we may call it so, is inhabited by barbarians, in distinct provinces and nations. . . .

They exceed one hundred and fifty, all with different languages. These nations are so near each other, that from the last villages of one they hear the people of the other at work. But this proximity does not lead to peace; on the contrary, they are engaged in constant wars, in which they kill and take prisoners great numbers of souls every day. This is the drain provided for so great a multitude, without which the whole land would not be large enough to hold them.

But though, among themselves, they are so warlike, none of them shewed courage to face Spaniards, as I observed throughout the voyage, in which the Indians never dared to use any defense against us, except that of flight. They navigate in vessels so light that, landing, they carry them on their shoulders, and, conveying them to one of the numerous lakes near the river, laugh at any enemy who, with heavier vessels, is unable to follow the same example. . . .

All those who live on the shores of this great river are collected in large villages, and, like the Venetians and Mexicans, their means of communication are by water, in small vessels which they call canoes. They are usually of cedar wood, which the providence of God abundantly supplies, without the labour of cutting it or carrying it from the forest; sending it down with the current of the river, which, to supply their wants, tears the trees from the most distant Cordilleras of Peru, and places them at the doors of their habitations, where each Indian may choose the piece of wood which suits him best. . . .

The rites of all these infidels are almost the same. They worship idols which they make with their own hands; attributing power over the waters to some, and, therefore, place a fish in their hands for distinction; others they choose as lords of the harvests; and others as gods of their battles. They say that these gods came down from Heaven to be their companions, and to do them good. They do not use any ceremony in worshipping them, and often leave them forgotten in a corner, until the time when they become necessary; thus when they are going to war, they carry an idol in the bows of their canoes, in which they place their hopes of victory; and when the go out fishing, they take the idol which is charged with dominion over the waters; but they do not trust in the one or the other so much as not to recognize another mightier God.

I gathered this from what happened with one of these Indians, who having heard something of the power of our God, and seen with his own eyes that our expedition went up the river, and, passing through the midst of so many warlike nations, returned without receiving any damage; judged that it was through the force and power of the God who guided us. He, therefore, came with much anxiety to beseech the captain and ourselves, that, in return for the hospitality he had shown us, we would leave him one of our gods, who would protect him and his people in peace and safety, and assist them to procure all necessary provisions. There were not wanting those who wished to console him by leaving in his village the standard of the cross, a thing which the Portuguese were accustomed to do among the infidels, not with so good a motive as would appear from the action itself. The sacred wood of the cross served to give color to the greatest injustice, such as the continual slavery of the poor Indians, whom, like meek lambs, they carried in flocks to their houses, to sell some, and treat the others with cruelty. These Portuguese raise the cross, and in payment of the kind treatment of the natives when they visit their villages, they fix it in the most conspicuous place, charging the Indians always to keep it intact. By some accident, or through the lapse of time, or purposely because these infidels do not care for it, the cross falls. Presently the Portuguese pass sentence, and condemn all the inhabitants of the village to perpetual slavery, not only for their lives, but for the lives of all their descendants.

For this reason I did not consent that they should plant the holy cross; and also that it might not give the Indian, who had asked us for a god, occasion for idolatry, by attributing to the wood the power of the Deity who redeemed us. . . .

It is worthy of notice that they all hold their sorcerers in very great estimation, not so much on account of the love they bear them, as for the dread in which they always live of the harm they are able to do them. These sorcerers usually have a house, where they practice their superstitious rites, and speak to the demon; and where, with a certain kind of veneration, the Indians keep all the bones of dead sorcerers, as if they were relics of saints. They suspend these bones in the same hammocks in which the sorcerers had slept when alive.

These men are their teachers, their preachers, their councilors, and their guides. They assist them in their doubts, and the Indians report to them in their wars, that they may receive poisonous herbs with which to take vengeance on their enemies. . . .

After having bathed with its waters a distance of thirteen hundred and fifty-six leagues of longitude, after sustaining on its banks an infinite number of barbarous tribes, after fertilizing vast territories, and after having passed through the centre of Peru, and, like a principal channel, collected the largest and richest of all its affluents, it [the Amazon] renders its tribute to the ocean.

Such is the sum of the new discovery of this great river, which excludes no one from its vast treasures, but rewards all who wish to take advantage of them. To the poor it offers sustenance, to the labourer a reward for his work, to the merchant employment, to the soldier opportunities to display his valour, to the rich an increase to his wealth, to the noble honours, to the powerful estates, and to the king himself a new empire.

SUGAR WAS KING (1654)

Sugar was the first of several agricultural products which would help mold the life of Brazil, first and most importantly its economy, but also its social structure, its politics, its literature, and other aspects. The north coastal sugar industry would later give way to the hegemony of coffee farther south, and the economic and political center of gravity would move southward with that agricultural shift, but for many years sugar was king. At other times cotton and, for a brief and meteoric episode, rubber would have great impact on Brazilian life, but in the beginning sugar ruled.

The following brief description of that industry is taken from a book by an English traveler, Richard Flecknoe, A Relation of Ten Years Travells in Europe, Asia, Affrique, and America (London: author, 1654).

I will return to speak of the Riches of the Country, chiefly consisting in their Sugar, which when I have named, I have named all; not that it wants others, but that it can want no others, having that, since that country which abounds with that commodity which all others have need of, can never want any commodity which others abound withall. . . . Now for their Sugar thus it grows, and thus 'tis made; Their Sugar canes are prun'd to the heighth of standing corn: nor need they other culture, but every second year to cut them close by the roots, as we do Osiers, when against the next year they never fail to spring up agen, the flaggs of which Canes are of a pleasant green, and shew a far off just like in a Field of Corn, which being ripe about the month of June, they joint them in pieces some foot long, and carry them to the Mill, turn'd by Oxen, or Water, consisting of two round Cylinders, about the bignesse of Mil-posts, plated with Iron, which turning inwards, and joyning as close together as they can meet, so squeez the canes in passing through them, as they come out on th' other side all bruzed, and dry as keques, which were all liquid before; which Liquor is conveyed by Troughs to certain Caldrons, where 'tis boyl'd, still retaining its amber colour, till pour'd out at last into their forms or coolers, with a certain Lee 'tis rendered white; And in these Mills (during the season of making Sugar) they work both day and night, the work of immediately applying the canes into the Mill being so perillous as if through drousinesse or heedlessnesse a fingers end be but engag'd betwixt the posts, their whole body inevitably follows, to prevent which, the next Negro has always a Hatchet readie to chop off his Arm, if any such Misfortune should arrive.

THE TREATY OF MADRID (1750)

The arbitrary and artificial lines drawn between Portuguese
and Spanish New World possessions, first by the Pope in 1493 and
second by bilateral treaty agreement between the two powers in
1494, were recognized from an early date to be unrealistic. The
bandeirante expeditions from São Paulo into the interior, which
continued for some two centuries, consolidated Portuguese de
facto possession of vast areas to the west of the Tordesillas (or Tordesilhas) line. In the middle of the eighteenth century, consequently, Portugal and Spain negotiated what one of the
foremost authorities on Brazilian history has called "one of the
most important documents in Brazilian history," the Treaty of
Madrid (1750), which established a Portuguese-Spanish boundary
in South America much in the location of the present boundary
between Brazil and its neighbors. As the treaty itself set out, it
established two important boundary criteria: reliance on natural
landmarks ("the sources and courses of rivers, and the most
remarkable mountains") and recognition of the status uti pos-
sidetis, i.e., that actual possession is "nine points in the law."
The second, in particular, worked greatly to Brazil's advantage.
    Though the Treaty of Madrid was a highly important one it did
not finally settle Brazil's boundaries. The Portuguese-Spanish
delimitation in South America was further modified in 1777. The
independence of the South American states in the early decades
of the nineteenth century greatly complicated the problems of
boundaries by substituting, ultimately, ten national flags for the
two (with the exception of the Guianas) which had flown over South
American during the colonial centuries. In the nineteenth and
twentieth centuries Brazil negotiated peaceful boundary settlements with all her abutting neighbors and in all instances, chiefly
by reason of very carefully prepared legal cases, she enlarged
her territory at the expense of those neighbors.
    The extract dealing with the Treaty of Madrid is taken from
the Statement Submitted by the United States of Brazil to
the President of the United States of America (New York: Knick-
erbocker Press, 1894).

The Most Serene Kings of Portugal and Spain, wishing effectively
to consolidate and make closer the sincere and cordial friendship they
profess for each other, have considered that the means most conducive
to the attainment of so salutary a purpose are to remove all pretexts
and clear away all impediments that may in future impair it, and particularly such as may arise with reference to the Boundaries in America
of the two Crowns, whose Conquests have advanced with uncertainty and
doubt, because, until now, the true Boundaries of those Dominions, or
the position in which must be imagined the Divisional Line, which was to

be the unalterable principle of the demarcation for both Crowns, have
not been ascertained. And considering the invincible difficulties which
would arise if this Line had to be marked with the requisite practical
knowledge, they have resolved to examine the reasons and uncertainties
that may be urged by both parties, and, in view of them, to conclude an
agreement to their mutual satisfaction and convenience.

On the part of the Crown of Portugal it was alleged that, inasmuch
as it was to reckon the one hundred and eighty degrees of its demarcation from the Line to the East, the other one hundred and eighty to
the West remaining for Spain; and while each one of the Nations was to
make its discoveries and establish its Colonies within one hundred and
eighty degrees of its demarcation; nevertheless it is found that, according
to the most exact and recent observations of Astronomers and Geographers,
beginning to count the degrees to the West of the said Line, the Spanish
Dominion at the Asiatic extremity of the South Sea extends to many more
degrees than the one hundred and eighty of its demarcation; and that
consequently it has occupied a much larger space than any excess at-
tributed to the Portuguese can amount to in that which perhaps they may
have occupied in South America to the West of the same Line, and at
the beginning of the Spanish demarcation.

It was also alleged that by the Deed of Sale with an agreement as to
repurchase (com pacto de retrovendendo) entered into by the Attorneys
of the two Crowns at Saragossa on the 22d of April, 1529, the Crown of
Spain sold to the Crown of Portugal all that by whatsoever means or right
appertained to it to the West of another imaginary Meridian Line, through
the Velas Islands [Marianas or Ladrone Islands], situated in the South
Sea, at a distance of 17 from Maluco [Moluccas or Spice Islands], with
the declaration that if Spain allowed and did not prevent its subjects from
navigating to the Westward of the said Line, then the agreement as to
repurchase should at once be rescinded and become void; and that when
any Spanish subjects, through ignorance or through necessity, should
pass within the Line, and discover any islands or lands, whatever might
be so discovered should belong to Portugal. That notwithstanding this
convention, the Spaniards subsequently proceeded to discover the Philip-
pines and, if fact, settled therein shortly before the union of the two
Crowns, which took place in the year 1580, and on account of which the
controversies between the two Nations caused by this contravention
ceased; but when they had again separated, the conditions of the Deed
of Saragossa gave rise to a new title by which Portugal may claim restitution of or equivalent for all that the Spanairds had occupied to the
West of said Line, in violation of that which had been capitulated in the
aforesaid Deed.

As to the Territory of the Northern bank of the River Plate, it was
alleged that, because of the foundation of the Colônia do Sacramento, a
controversy arose between the two Crowns, relative to Boundaries: that
is to say, as to whether the lands upon which that fortress was built, were
to the East or to the West of the Boundary Line agreed upon in Tordesilhas
[the Portuguese form of Tordesillas]; and, while this question was being
decided, a provisional Treaty was concluded at Lisbon on the 7th of May,
1681, by which it was agreed that the aforesaid fortress should remain

in the possession of the Portuguese; and that they should have in common with the Spaniards the use and benefit of the lands in dispute. That by Article VI of the Treaty of peace, concluded at Utrecht between the two Crowns, on the 6th of February, 1715, His Catholic Majesty ceded all action and right he may have had to Colônia and its Territory, the Provisonal Treaty being abolished by virtue of cession. That whereas by virtue of the same cession the whole of the disputed Territory was to be delivered to the Crown of Portugal, the Governor of Buenos-Ayres contrived to surrender only the fortress, saying that by Territory he only understood what was within cannon-shot of it, reserving to the Crown of Spain all the other lands in dispute, on which was afterwards founded the Fortress of Montevideo and other establishments: That this interpretation of the Governor of Buenos-Ayres was manifestly opposed to what had been agreed, it being evident that the Crown of Spain, by means of its own cession, could not be placed in a better position than that in which it was before, in regard to the same thing that it had ceded; and that both Nations, having by the Provisional Treaty been left in common possession and enjoyment of those Plains, there is no more violent interpretation than to suppose that, by means of the cession of His Catholic Majesty, they were vested exclusively in his Crown.

That inasmuch as that Territory belongs to Portugal by a title different from that of the Boundary Line defined at Tordesilhas (that is to say, by the agreement made in the Treaty of Utrecht, in which His Catholic Majesty ceded his right under the old demarcation), such Territory ought, independently of questions concerning that Line, to be entirely surrendered to Portugal, together with everything which might newly have been built upon it, as having been erected upon foreign soil. Lastly that, assuming that His Catholic Majesty had reserved the right of offering an equivalent, to the satisfaction of His Most Faithful Majesty, for the said Colônia and its Territory, nevertheless as many years had elapsed since the expiration of the terms fixed for this offer, every pretext or motive, even apparent, for delaying the cession of the same Territory has ceased to exist.

On the part of the Crown of Spain it was alleged that as a Line from North to South was to be imagined three hundred and seventy leagues West of the Cape Verde Islands, in accordance with the Treaty concluded at Tordesilhas on the 7th of June, 1494, all the land that might lie within the three hundred and seventy leagues from the said islands to the place where the Line ought to be laid down, belongs to Portugal, and nothing more in this direction; because the one hundred and eighty degrees of the demarcation of Spain must be reckoned thence Westward: and, although, because it is not stated from which of the Cape Verde Islands the three hundred and seventy leagues are to be reckoned, a doubt has arisen, and this point is of great interest, seeing that they are all situated East and West with a difference of four and a half degrees; it is certain also that, even if Spain yielded, and consented that the reckoning should begin from the most Westerly, which is named Santo Antão, the three hundred and seventy leagues would scarcely extend as far as the City of Pará, and other Colonies, or Portuguese Captaincies founded formerly on the coasts of Brazil; and as the Crown of Portugal has occupied the two banks of

the River Amazonas, or Marañón, up as far as the mouth of the River
Javarí, which flows into it by the Southern bank, it clearly follows that
it has encroached upon the territory of the Spanish demarcation to the
extent of the distance of the said City from the mouth of the said river,
the same being the case in the interior of Brazil with regard to the advance inward made by this Crown to Cuyabá and Matto Grosso.

With regard to Colônia do Sacramento, it was alleged that, according to the most accurate Maps, the place at which the Line ought to be
imagined does not reach by a long distance the mouth of the River Plate;
and, consequently, the said Colônia with all its Territory lies to the West
of it, and within the boundary of Spain, without prejudice to the new right
under which the Crown of Portugal retains it by virtue of the Treaty of
Utrecht, since restitution by an equivalent was stipulated therein; and
although the Court of Spain offered the equivalent within the period prescribed by Article VII, that of Portugal did not accept it: on which account
the period was extended, the equivalent being, as it was, proportionate;
and the not having admitted it was more though the fault of Portugal than
that of Spain.

These reasons having been seen and examined by the two Most
Serene Monarchs with the replications that were made on both sides,
proceeding with that good faith and sincerity which is so becoming in
Princes so just, so friendly, and who are related, wishing to maintain
their Subjects in peace and quietness, and recognizing the difficulties
and doubts which in all time would complicate this controversy, if it had
to be decided by means of the demarcation adjusted in Tordesilhas, both
because it was not stated from which of the Cape Verde Islands the three
hundred and seventy leagues was to be reckoned, and on account of the
difficulty of determining on the coasts of South America the two points
on the South and North from which the Line was to begin; on account, also,
of the moral impossibility of establishing accurately through the center
of the same America a Meridian Line; and, lastly, on account of many
other almost insurmountable difficulties which would occur in the way
of preserving without controversy or encroachment a demarcation regulated by Meridian Lines; and considering at the same time that the said
difficulties were perhaps in the past the chief cause of the encroachments
set out by both parties, and of the numerous conflicts which disturbed the
peace of their Dominions; they have resolved to put an end to past and
future disputes, and to forget and desist from all actions and rights that
they may have by virtue of the said Treaties of Tordesilhas, Lisbon,
Utrecht, and the Deed of Saragossa, or of any other grounds whatever
which may influence them in the division of their Dominions by a Meridian
Line; and it is their will that for the future the same shall not be further
considered, the Boundaries of the two Monarchies being reduced to those
which are specified in the present Treaty, it being their desire that two
purposes shall be carefully secured by it: The first, and principal one is
that the Boundaries of the two Dominions shall be defined, taking as
landmarks the best known spots, so that they may never be mistaken or
give rise to disputes, such as the sources and courses of rivers, and the
most remarkable mountains: The second, that each party shall remain
in possession of that which it holds at the present time, with the exception

of mutual cessions, which shall be mentioned in the proper place; which cessions shall be carried out for mutual convenience, and in order that the Borders may be as little subject to controversy as possible.

THE SECRET INSTRUCTIONS OF VICEROY LAVRADIO TO HIS SUCCESSOR (1779)

The appointment in 1750 of the Marquis of Pombal as principal minister of the Portuguese king was followed by a general tightening of colonial administration. Pombal had a worthy subordinate in the Marquis of Lavradio, viceroy of Brazil for a decade beginning in 1769. On learning of his replacement, the viceroy wrote a secret letter of information and instructions to his successor giving in detail an account of the status and problems of the colony. It is noteworthy not only as a revelation of the constructive contributions made by a conscientious administrator, but also as a commentary on the shortcomings of lower officials as well as of merchants and planters.

The letter was published in a volume by John Armitage, The History of Brazil (London: Smith, Adam and Co., 1836).

Although the brilliant acquirements and distinguished talents of your Excellency may easily recognize whatever is of most importance in this Captaincy, and though your penetration may discover whatever be immediately necessary, by your inquiries, without the aid of the following diffuse and incomplete narration; yet as there may be some particulars with which you might for a long time be unacquainted, and towards which your attention will be required, in order that your cares and judicious measures may remedy my errors, the love which I bear to the royal service, and the interest which I take in the good of this people and in the good of the State, induce me to lay before your Excellency a narration of the forces of this Captaincy, -- of the state in which I found it, -- of its interests, -- of the system which I have followed, -- of the character of its inhabitants, and lastly, of the state in which I deliver it over to your Excellency. And if this my narration do not satisfy all the curiosity of your Excellency, you will be pleased to excuse me on account of this document being original, i.e. that I am the first who give an account to my successor of the Government which I deliver to him; this ceremony never having been before attended with any other formality than that of reading the Patents, or "Cartas Regias," of their Majesties to the individuals appointed, and to those deposed. This was all the instruction which I myself received, and I was thus obliged to lose much time ere I could trace out a path in which I could travel with perspicuity.

. . .

I found the troops in good order as far as regards evolutions, and that they were well provided for, but I found the jurisdiction materially altered, since the Lieutenant-General had overstretched his authority. The Viceroys were dissatisfied, but they permitted his usurpations and vented their spleen only in complaints, for which he cared but little. He acted with asperity towards the troops and his officers, and carried into execution the regulations even in points wherein they are prejudicial in this country, both to the life of men and to the State. Now the season for exercise selected in Europe on account of the coolness of the weather, is in America the hottest period of the year, and is also the rainy season, from which cause I found many sick, that many others had lost their lives, and that others again has thus contracted maladies which had disabled them for the service. He consented to no more marriages than were permitted by the terms of the regulations, and as the armed force comprehends a great number of people in this country, he thus checked the means which might concur to the augmentation of the State. This excess of jurisdiction on the part of the Lieutenant-General, the consequent discontent of the Viceroy, the severity with which the troops were treated, and their loss of life and health, had given rise to so much intrigue and partiality, that every thing was in the greatest confusion, and there were so many deserters, that from these various motives the regiments were much diminished.

.   .   .

That district is a highly important one, and worthy of the particular attention of your Excellency; its immense plains are extremely fertile, and the sugar-cane and all kinds of vegetables flourish there. It has also much excellent timber, admirable balsams, oils, and gums, and many other precious drugs, with all of which commerce might be increased. It also possesses excellent mines of gold, which may be of great utility to the State when His Majesty shall be informed of their situation, and permit them to be worked by the people. It has many navigable rivers in which even now a good commerce is carried on. For many years it was the general asylum of all malefactors, thieves, and assassins, who sought refuge there, and were allowed so much liberty that they felt no actual subjection; but lived in idleness, cultivating no more than was necessary for their subsistence. It has been extremely difficult to reduce them to order. I found, however, that this had been facilitated by the Viceroys, my predecessors, and by following in their steps both commerce and agriculture have increased under my government, as your Excellency will see from the annexed relation of the Colonel of Militia; but as these people have had such a bad education, it is necessary for the present to avoid giving them any power or authority, which may fill them with vanity, and lead to disastrous consequences.

I have followed the system of conceding many grants of land to people of this Capital who go to settle there, -- I have sent for many of the inhabitants here, that I might speak to them, -- I have retained them here for some time, in order that they might be witnesses of a people living in a state of subjection, and that they might observe what respect and obedience is paid to the magistrates, and other individuals in authority; and during all the time that they have remained here I have made them feel their dependencies as much as possible. Finally, when I have again sent them away, I have always rendered them some benefit, and they have thus been gradually civilized in such a manner that those horrible disorders, which were once a daily source of disquietude to the Governors of this Captaincy, have no longer existence.

The greatest care ought to be taken that no attorneys, public writers, or other people of unquiet spirits, go to establish themselves there, since as the people have had a bad education, no sooner do they hear any turbulent individuals flattering them, and inciting them to insolence, than they immediately forget their duty, and range themselves under his banners. In my time this occurred in the case of an Advocate, José Pereira, who appearing to me a pacific character, and in good circumstances, I made Judge relative to the grants of land. He, however, became the cause of such disorders, that even a revolt took place; in which, if I had not had recourse to extraordinary measures, the farms and establishments in progress there might have been utterly destroyed. I immediately sent for both this man and the individuals with whom he was in dispute, I threw them into a close prison, and treated them with the utmost severity, and with this proceeding intimidated the rest. Afterwards, on tranquility being restored, I allowed them to return, in order that they might inform others how they had been treated, telling them at the same time, that in case of any further disturbances, I should make them responsible for every thing that occurred, so that they have henceforth taken the office of peacemakers, and quiet has been maintained.

I hope your Excellency will excuse me for having dilated on this head; but as I consider that district as one of the most important, I have deemed it requisite to do this, in order that your Excellency may be fully acquainted with its condition.

Of all these battalions, detachments were during the war sent to this Capital, and with these the fortresses were garrisoned. I also availed myself of this occasion to exercise the troops; and all the militia thus became qualified to serve efficiently in case of any attack. I ought also to inform your Excellency that I have had another still more cogent reason for bringing into the militia all the able-bodied men, and into the Ordenanças all such as are disabled; and this is to reduce these people in small divisions, under the command of respectable individuals appointed as their officers, and to keep these again in such subordination, that all may recognize the due authority of the person appointed by His Majesty to the government of this vast, prolific, and rich country, inhabited for the most part by people devoid of education, licentious in character, heterogeneous in caste, and unaccustomed to any subjection except to the Government and Magistrates. Unless, in the first instance, they be separated, and made to rcognize other and more immediate superiors, who (though themselves the depositaries of the laws and orders of the Sovereign), give an example of obedience and respect, it is quite impossible to govern without disturbance.

Experience has shown this, since, in all the points where there has been neglect in reducing the people to this system, the disorders and tumults have been frequent, and not even the penalty of death has been able to diminish them; whereas, in all points where the system has been adopted, tranquility has been maintained, disorders are less frequent, and the laws are more respected. I make these reflections, since your Excellency will find much opposition to the conservation of these corps.

The Lieutenant-General has the greatest envy of them; for, without looking to their great utility, he is vexed to see men who are not soldiers in uniform, and desires to see a distinction made between their officers and those of the regular troops, without remembering that the former serve without remuneration. Many private individuals, also, who desire to live in liberty, and free from subjection, employ all the means in their power to throw off a yoke which is necessary for their own good.

.   .   .

Having hitherto spoken to your Excellency relative to the situation and military forces of the Captaincy, I shall now proceed to treat of the political and civil body, the character of the people, and the system which I have followed. Your Excellency has the Court of Appeal, and the Magistrates composing it. Up to the present time its members have fulfilled their obligations in a distinguished manner, and I have had no complaints whatever of want of rectitude in their decisions. In this Capital there is also an Ouvidor [a special magistrate] and a Juiz de Fora [a circuit judge]. The Ouvidor, besides being of very limited capacity, has, by old age and ill health, been totally disqualified for the performance of the duties of his office. As he is not sufficiently strong to fulfil his obligations, he frequently employs Advocates to execute his tasks, and it has thus happened on several occasions that the same Advocate who has been employed by the defendant, has, on the other hand, acted as accuser, and subsequently passes sentence as Judge. The consequences of such proceedings must be clearly apparent to your Excellency, yet the whole is managed with so much art that it is almost impossible to authenticate the fact, since the Advocates signing law papers on the part of the Ouvidor cause the papers of their clients to be signed by other Advocates, who thus earn a livelihood; and it is thus impossible either to prove or to rectify the irregularity. I however make your Excellency acquainted with the circumstance, in order that you may adopt the measures which you deem the most expedient. The Juiz de Fora, at present here, bears a good character. A Judge for criminal causes is much wanted in this city, as your Excellency will afterwards see.

Some more Juizes de Fora are also necessary, and especially one for the district of Santo Antônio de Sá and the neighbourhood, -- another for Campos dos Goitacazes, -- another for the island of St. Catharine, and another for Rio Grande de San Pedro; it being necessary, before the nomination of these magistrates, that a scrupulous examination be instituted relative to their worth and talents. A knowledge of the laws and civil jurisprudence is not sufficient; they ought to be endowed with patriotism, and of a disposition which may give hope that they will endeavour to promote the prosperity and happiness of the people, both in appeasing their differences, animating their commerce and agriculture, and in opposing the sloth and erroneous prejudices which have led to the utmost indigence. The three Ouvidores required, viz., the one for this Capital, the one for the Captaincy of Espirito Santo and Campos, and the one for St. Catharine and Rio Grande, ought to be three active men who will carry through the beneficial measures already commenced by the Juizes de Fora of these districts. Without these magistrates, your Excellency will find it difficult to accomplish the augmentation and prosperity of this Captaincy. I have laboured nearly two years for this object; I have been tenacious, and I have not been checked by the doubts and difficulties which every instant presented themselves, yet as I have wanted support, I have done but little. In general the magistrates who come to this country (as far as my experience goes), think of nothing further than fulfilling the time for which they have been sent here, in order that they may afterwards claim promotion; and during the time of their residence, their only study is to accumulate all that they can, in order that on their return they may benefit their families. Not one of them speaks of the utility of which he has been, or of any useful establishment which he has aided: all bewail the misery and poverty of their districts, being moved to this compassion by the trifling revenue which they have drawn from their office.

As the salaries of these magistrates are small, their chief aim is not to retire, some with less property than others, and they seek to multiply their emoluments by litigation and discord, which they foment, and not only keep the people unquiet, but put them to heavy expenses, and divert them from their occupations, with the end of promoting their own vile interest and that of their subalterns, who are the principal concocters of these disorders. During nearly twelve years that I have governed in America, I never heard speak of a single Judge who endeavoured to recon-cile litigants, -- persuading them not to ruin themselves by continued and unjust pleas, and who did in this respect what is so often recommended in the laws themselves. I may also state that I never found any one useful establishment instituted by any of these magistrates, and having sent to several of them to obtain information on a matter of this kind, I found them so ignorant and unacquainted with all such topics, that I resolved never more to have any conferences with them. Being in the end convinced of these truths, and aware that I ought to interfere, I endeavoured on numberless occasions to become the mediator between contending parties, no matter whether poor or rich, labourers or merchants; I called them mutually into my presence and reconciled them, and others I induced to appoint arbitrators for the adjustment of their differences; and in this manner, in the shortest way, I endeavour to cause them to live together quietly, and to prevent them from ruining each other. Certainly the magis-trates complained that law-suits were fewer and that their places were worth less than before; but the people experienced the benefit; commerce and labour increased, and would have increased still more if the said Judges had not opposed my efforts by all the means in their power.

Unless your Excellency, in the absence of any further orders from his Majesty on this point, do not pursue the same system with myself, you may rely upon it, this Capital will be ruined in a very short time, since as soon as it is known that your Excellency will leave every thing to the judicial tribunals, new law-suits will arise every instant, many that are now regarded as at an end, will begin again; the Magistracy who can now accumulate little more than will suffice to pay their passage to the mother country, will again be enabled to enrich themselves as formerly, but the people will be ruined.

.   .   .

To avoid the recurrence of these abuses, I ordered that the coffer should be conveyed to the Mint, that the Treasurer should find sureties, that there should be certain days of payment, and that a code of regulations which I framed should be executed. Accordingly the state of the coffer is always known, individuals receive the amount of deposits immediately, and all loss is prevented. I gave in an account of all this to the Marquis de Pombal: and receiving no answer, I persisted in my decisions.

There was, moreover, in this city a terrible nuisance, occasioned by the Negroes arriving from the coast of Africa. As soon as they were disembarked they entered the city by the principal streets, though not only covered with filthy diseases, but naked, and being devoid of all instructions, they were in the habit of enacting the most disgusting scenes in the streets, before the houses where they were stationed. Respectable people could not appear with decency at the windows, and yet the abuse was permitted under pretext that the owners of the slaves were spared expense of rent by exposing them in the street by day, and bringing them into their dwellings by night. This disorderly proceedings, it cost me a great deal of trouble to obviate, and nothing but the most extreme constancy enabled me to succeed.

My resolution was, that on slaves being disembarked in the Customhouse, they should again be sent in boats to the Valongo (which is apart from all the rest of the city), and that they should there be deposited in stores, or warehouses. Also, I decided, that the purchasers should never enter with more than four or five naked slaves into the city, and that those bought for the province of Minas, or for the plantations, should be retained in the square of St. Domingos, where there was every convenience for the object, until they were taken away from the city.

I paid a great deal of attention to the execution of this order, and, although with difficulty, I caused it to be carried into effect, the health of the inhabitants of the city improved, the slaves themselves were more easily cured of their maladies, and to-day all acknowledge the beneficial result of what I have done. The slave-owners, nevertheless, do everything in their power to bring affairs into their former train -- regarding their complaints, your Excellency will act as you think proper.

I have now spoken to your Excellency of the military, political, and civil state of this capital, and have now only to address you regarding the character of the people, the merchants, their commerce, and my system of government. The general character of the inhabitants of those parts of America with which I am acquainted, is that of indolence, humility, and obedience. They are sober in their habits, yet they have at the same time great vanity and hauteur; but these defects are easily subdued. They are robust, support labor well, and follow the commands they receive; yet, unless they be commanded, they often remain in a state of inaction, until they are reduced to the most extreme indigence. Yet these very individuals, who are by themselves very easy to govern, sometimes become unmanageable, and give a great deal of trouble, on account of the Europeans, who have their establishments here.

.   .   .

Those who are here regarded as the richest merchants, as, for instance, Braz Carneiro Leão, Manoel de Costa Cardozo, José Caetano Alvez, and some others, have acquired their riches by commissions, and the consignment of vessels. As these men are very active, and have generally disposed of the merchandize sent to them, on good terms, and been diligent in procuring cargoes for their vessels, they are in good repute in Europe, and have thus acquired their capital. Though, however, these men are both rich and honourable, I cannot regard their houses as commercial houses, since they themselves are ignorant of their profession, and of the most approved methods of bookkeeping. At present, since the establishment of a commercial school, some clerks have been found who have put their books to better order; but this is only in a few instances. As these men are simple commission agents, they cannot forward the commerce of the State; since they are bound by the orders of their constituents, and can ship nothing without instructions. The exports thus consist exclusively of commodities which have been known for years, and all others are neglected. The commission agents here will not send any new commodities, since they have no orders for them, and they are too timid to send them on their own account. Thus your Excellency will perceive that, for the augmentation of the commerce of this Captaincy, the establishment of companies with partners, both in Brazil and in Europe, is necessary, or a more scrutinizing policy on the part of the merchants of Europe. Otherwise, it is impossible that commerce should increase, and your Excellency will have the disgust of seeing many precious and available articles of export utterly neglected. It was always my system, on all these points, to consider that every thing relating to the felicity, comfort, defence, and protection of these people, was my charge, and that I had a jurisdiction to interfere in all the foregoing departments, and take such measures as I regarded most conducive to the above ends.

In the municipal chamber I allowed the President and the Aldermen to govern according to their attributes, I meanwhile paying attention to all irregularities, and writing from time to time to the chamber to remind its members of their obligations. These my determinations or hints were, however, always ordered to be executed in the name of the chamber. I always followed the system of taking no notice whatever of the murmurs of the people. I always endeavoured to ascertain, without their perceiving it, when they were really aggrieved, and when I considered that they were, I endeavoured, as though insensibly, to amend my own resolutions, but always remained constant in my designs, feigning myself ignorant of what was said. Often, under other pretexts, I gave the complainants an opportunity of speaking to me, and, after having conversed with them freely, without allowing them to suppose me aware of their complaints, I led to the topic which had excited them, and, after repeating the objections which might be urged against my plans, I proceeded to answer them in such a natural manner, that they became convinced that I was right, and, being disabused, they imagined that I had chosen them for my confidants, never suspecting my real motives. As the good of the people has ever been my chief object, I endeavoured by all the means possible to avoid all prejudice to them, and at the same time to benefit their credit and reputation.

From what I have here said, your Excellency will perceive that His Majesty ought to be immediately made aware of the want of means in this Captaincy, both for the payment of the old debt, and the annual expenses. The public expenses increase daily, and the voluntary subsidy, the voluntary revenue, and the revenue arising from the estates of the Jesuits have ceased. Other branches of the revenue, as those of the Chancellorship and the duties on wines, have diminished and others, such as the contract for the whale-fishery, and for salt, which ought to have doubled, have been lately sold at only a slight advance. Unless, indeed, some measures be taken for the relief of the Captaincy, your Excellency must necessarily contract a further debt of from 200,000 to 300,000 cruzados annually, and thus contribute to cripple commerce, and to depress industry still further.

The culpable negligence of the Secretary of the Junta, João Carlos Correia de Lemos, in conjunction with the malice which at times induced him to revenge himself on those who have complained of his delays, has prevented me from being enabled to draw out a formal account of the matter, fit to be presented to his Majesty. It has, moreover, appeared to me, that the statement ought to be presented in the name of the Junta de Fazenda, on account of its being the tribunal entrusted with the administration of this object. Not only, however, has the above-mentioned Secretary prevented this being done, but, by his idleness and the confused manner in which he keeps his accounts, he has been more than a year and a half in drawing out the accounts of the expenditure, since the commencement of the war, of the revenue during this time, of what we owe, and of what we are owed by the other Captaincies, according to what they ought to remit us, in conformity with the royal orders. Indispensable as is all this, I could never cause him to do it.

From what I have had the honour to say to your Excellency, you must perceive that I could not adhere to any fixed system; yet my chief objects were the preservation of the people in tranquility and obedience, the promotion of their good, the arousing them from idleness, and the promotion of the interests of His Majesty; and, although I could never do what I wished from a want of means, I succeeded to a certain extent. I promoted the tranquility and obedience of the people by the means already indicated; I promoted their good by forcibly compelling them to plant those products which are chiefly necessary for subsistence, such as maize and pulse; I threatened to take away their lands from them, unless they cultivated them diligently; I compelled the Colonels of Militia to give in exact statements on this matter, and thus led to a great increase both of these productions and of sugar. I promoted the culture of rice, and induced various merchants to assist and animate the labourers planters; in consequence, this article, which it was a short time ago necessary to purchase in Europe, is now so abundant that it is exported. I also forcibly compelled them to plant a portion of indigo, which was a shrub which grew uselessly in the forests, and for which nobody cared; and at the same time while I obliged them to cultivate it, I caused other to prepare the plant, paying them, however, for the indigo when prepared. In this manner I gave a material impulse to the cultivation of a new branch of commerce; but as it was a product little known, the merchants were afraid to purchase it,

and as they offered but very low prices to the cultivators, it again retro-
graded. I stated all this to the Court, and His Majesty was pleased to
order the quality of the indigo to be examined and divided into three classes,
on each of which there was to be an established price, and that the whole
should be purchased by the royal Treasury at the established rates, and
no private individuals permitted to purchase the article. This was accordingly done; but I found that the expense might often exceed the resources
of the Treasury, and the payments to the cultivators might thus be delayed,
and the culture retarded. I also recollected that when people are obliged
to dispose of an article to the royal Treasury, at stipulated prices, they
always feel irritated, from a belief that they could obtain more from private
individuals, and this might also be an inducement to abandon its cultivation.
On this account, I represented to His Majesty, that it appeared to me
that it would be well for the royal Treasury to make purchases; but that
I should also recommend the cultivators to be left at liberty to make the
best bargains possible with private individuals. They would thus be guaranteed from loss, since, when no private purchasers were found, the royal
Treasury would pay them at established prices. My anticipations were
verified; for, as the royal Treasury was straitened for means, payments
to the cultivators were often delayed without my being aware of it. Some
merchants also induced them to believe that they could give them higher
prices, and the result was so much vexation, that more than thirty cultivators abandoned this branch of industry altogether, and others prepared
to follow their example.

It appeared to me that, until I received an answer to my representation, I ought to permit some merchants to make purchases, not, however,
permitting that this should be done without my consent. They thus immediately began to purchase at higher rates than the Treasury, and the
cultivators were encouraged to proceed; but those who had abandoned the
business did not return to it. The merchants sent the indigo which they
had purchased to Lisbon; but as it there came into competition with a
quantity found in some prize vessels taken from the Spanairds, the price
fell very much, and a remunerating rate could no longer be given. Finally,
the last resolution of the Court arrived, whereby His Majesty gave the
cultivators permission either to dispose of it to whom they thought proper,
or to export it on their own account, and appointed, also, certain stipulated
prices to be paid for it at the royal Treasury. I published a proclamation
to this effect, and stated, that henceforward all cultivators would be re-
imbursed without the slightest delay, and that I myself would provide funds
for the object. The consequence was, that not only was a large quantity
bought, but the merchants again began to buy, and the cultivators, in some
instances, proceeded to export the article on their own account. It is only
thus, that commerce and agriculture can be promoted in these dominions.
Unless the Sovereign encourage and indemnify the cultivators, nothing
can be done; but your Excellency must be aware that these succours, far
from being prejudicial to the interests of His Majesty, on the contrary,
contribute to an increase of revenue.

About the same period, an individual named João Opmam brought
under my notice a plant called Guaxima, capable of making excellent
cordage and cables. It appeared to me, that this might be of the greatest

utility, and I resolved on commencing a series of experiments, which I have answered as well as could be anticipated. In the first instance, cables were made, but the plant was cut in the wrong season, and prepared by unskilful and ignorant individuals, and the cablemakers neither knew how to twist the thread nor to pitch it. I nevertheless caused some of them to be used in the vessels of the squadron, where they were found almost, if not quite as good, as those of hemp. I gave an account of this discovery to the Court, and, by order of His Majesty, some lengths of this rope were made for comparison with the cordage of Riga. It cannot, however, excite surprise that this cordage, the preparation of which was not understood, should have been found inferior to that of Riga, which is superior to all other qualities known, therefore, in order to make a fair comparison, I ordered a rope to be bought in one of the shops in the city, and the strength of it tried with one of Guaxima, and as your Excellency was present during the experiment, you will recollect what was the result. Previous to this, I had ordered the cultivation of the plant and had constructed a ropewalk. The cultivators of the plant I paid at so much an arroba, and charged João Opmam to receive it, and to pay them from funds furnished by the Royal Treasury. In the meantime I occupied him in making cordage for the public service, in which he has since been employed without any wages or recompense. I have permitted him to make and sell cordage to private individuals; but as he is very poor, he requires further encouragement, or the establishment must be abandoned. In consequence of the experiments made with these ropes, and those of Riga, the Court has decided in favor of the latter; yet, in the absence of a total prohibition, I have continued to promote the cultivation and production of the former, considering that, even in case of its inferiority, it may answer for ordinary purposes and in small vessels. The culture of this plant does not interfere with that of hemp. I have endeavoured to establish hemp also, but I had difficulty in procuring the seed, which I at last obtained in a casual manner from a French vessel, and which I ordered to be sowed with great care. The birds destroyed the greater part of the crop, but some seed was retained, and I sent it to the island of St. Catherine to be planted. At the time when the Spaniards invaded that island there were hopes of a plentiful crop, but all my hopes were frustrated. Having, however, heard, after the restitution of the island, that some persons had had the curiosity to preserve the seed, I ordered them to plant it again, in hope of realizing my former plans. I ought to inform your Excellency, that not only are there excellent situations for these plantations on the island of St. Catherine, but also in Rio Grande, Campos dos Goitacazes, and some places in the vicinity of the city, such as Santa Cruz.

. . .

The good sucess of mulberry trees in America induced me to make a plantation of them, and with great exertion I obtained silk-worms from Europe, which have multiplied abundantly. Some silk has been made, but my efforts to hit upon the best plan of raising the worm have been in vain. As this country has a similar climate to Asia, where the silk-worm succeeds, I have written there for instructions as to its treatment, but have not yet received an answer. When it arrives it will be placed in the hands of your Excellency. Francisco Xavier is at present entrusted with the mulberry plantation, and the care of the silk-worms, and from him all the information which your Excellency may require can be obtained.

From all the districts I have sent for timbers, oils, balsams, gums, and shrubs, which I have transmitted to the court, in order that their virtues might be ascertained, and commerce promoted. The Minister of State informed me that many have already been examined, and some excellent dyes have been found amongst them; but, ere they had written to me explicity on this point, the news arrived of my having the felicity to be substituted by your Excellency, and I therefore suspended all my measures under the certainty that your Excellency would act much more judiciously than I could. Such are the particulars of several of the plans which I attempted to carry into execution.

My self-love does not blind me to the point of inducing me to defend all my resolutions as judicious; I did what I could, and what my limited talents permitted me, and I never omitted any labours which appeared likely to prevent my falling into error. Your Excellency will act with more discretion, and, by correcting my imperfections and mistakes, will bring about that felicity of the people which I have ever desired, and still desire.

.   .   .

In the last place, it is neccessary that I speak to your Excellency regarding the conclusion of the treaty, which I ordered to be executed on receipt of the last orders from the Court. I named Jozé Marcelino as first Commissioner, and of this I informed the Spanish general. I named as Commissioner to take account of the prisoners, military stores, provisions and effects appertaining to His Majesty and his vassals, and taken by the Spaniards during the interim elapsing from the date of the Treaty of Paris in 1763 to the present time, -- Lieutenant-Colonel Vicente Jozé de Velasco Molina, and as his substitute Major Pedro de Silva. I requested from the General of Buenos Ayres, a counter-nomination, but as it was his object to delay the conclusion of the treaty, although it is far from being disadvantageous to him, he has evinced much bad faith and insincerity, procrastinating as much as possible, yet pretending that the delay occasioned was much against his inclination, in the face of evidence to the contrary. This your Excellency will see evinced in despatches and papers of Velasco, and the replies to them. With regard, however, to the demarcation of limits, nothing can be done at present from a want of means. In the first place, the instruments necessary for the operation are wanting, and, secondly, geographers are wanting to be divided and sub-divided into different companies. Many doubts will necessarily arise on account of the incorrectness of maps, and the formation of establishments in the interior will be necessary for the sustenance of the individuals employed. Your Excellency will perceive that I was devoid of all the necessary and indispensable means for the object: all that I could do was to nominate Jozé Marcelino as my first Commissioner, which nomination I made rather to satisfy the Spaniards in appearance, than with the idea of availing myself of his services. His pride and his incapacity alone unfit him for any office wherein sincerity is required, and his interference could lead only to continual doubts, discord, and embarrassment. Engineers and instruments are also wanting, and I was supplied only with orders from the Government. The opinion of Francisco João Rocio regarding the demarcation appears to me extremely correct, and I should recommend both him and the Colonel Rafael Pinto Bandeira to be employed on occasion of the demarcation. The latter is in fact so well versed in the geography of the country, that he may be said to have the map of it in his head. By means of these two men, the Court may be assured that all doubts will be resolved, while unless they be employed, difficulties will arise, time and money will be thrown away, and our sincerity will be distrusted.

What I have had the honour of repeating to your Excellency in the foregoing document, is what appears to me most essential regarding the present state of the Government, and regarding also what I have done. All my errors your Excellency will amend, with that wisdom and prudence which is characteristic of your distinguished talents, and thus will the people under your charge be enabled to enjoy all the good fortune possible, and your Excellency all the glory which I desire.

May God guard your Excellency.

(Signed) MARQUIS DE LAVRADIO

Rio de Janeiro,
19th of June, 1779,

THE SENTENCE OF TIRADENTES (1792)

For obvious reasons, the path toward independence followed by Brazil differed greatly from those taken by the Spanish colonies in Latin America. But both in Brazil and in the Spanish possessions there were manifestations of discontent in the late eighteenth century. The revolt, trial, and sentencing of Joaquim José da Silva Xavier, popularly known as Tiradentes (the Tooth-puller) in 1789-92 were more dramatic than significant, but the sentence on April 18, 1792, illustrates not only the incipient threat faced by Portuguese authority but also the severity of the more extreme punishments at times meted out.

The sentence was translated by Professor E. Bradford Burns from Lúcio José dos Santos, A Inconfidência Mineira (São Paulo: Escolas Profissionaes do Lyceu Coração de Jesus, 1927).

Therefore, they condemn the criminal Joaquim José da Silva Xavier, known as Tiradentes, formerly second lieutenant of the troops in Minas Gerais, to be paraded with hangman's noose and public proclamation through the public streets to the place of hanging, where he will be executed, and that after death his head will be cut off and taken to Villa Rica where in the most public place it will be fastened to a tall pole until consumed by time; his body will be divided into four quarters and fastened to poles along the road to Minas at Varginha and Sevolas, where the criminal carried on his infamous practices, and the rest at places of greatest population until consumed by time. They declare the criminal infamous and his sons and grandsons infamous and his goods confiscated and the house in which he lived in Villa Rica will be leveled and the ground salted so that nothing more can be built there; and if they do not belong to him, they will be appraised and the owner paid from the confiscated goods, and on that same spot will be placed a sign to preserve forever the infamy of this abominable criminal.

PORTUGUESE CHAINS ON THE BRAZILIAN ECONOMY (1794)

Portuguese economic policies toward her colonies were no more enlightened than those of other contemporary European states with colonial empires. It was all an inheritance from the application of mercantilist economic theory: in short, the colonies must be milked for the benefit of the mother country. In the Brazilian case the situation was well illustrated by an essay written by José Joaquim da Cunha de Azeredo Coutinho in 1794, extracts from which are given below. Azeredo Coutinho was Brazilian born but Portuguese educated. He put an unerring finger on the shortcomings and shortsightedness of Portuguese policy. The excerpts are taken from his An Essay on the Commerce and Products of the Portuguese Colonies in South America, Especially the Brazils (London: translator, 1807).

The salt trade being prohibited throughout Brazil, the exclusive privilege for this useful branch of commerce is farmed out to one individual, who pays for it the sum of 48,000,000 of Réis, every year, into the Royal treasury. This farmer gets annually from Brazil ninety-six millions of Réis, of which forty-eight millions go to the queen's treasury, and an equal sum remains for himself, his agents, and receivers, even after deducting all the principal expenses of the salt, including freight and carriage. But much more considerable are the profits he draws from the interparts of those districts, where the herds are more numerous, the demand for salt consequently greater, and the price of that article enhanced in proportion to the expense of carriage, over the many mountains, which are there to be met with.

On account of the vast sum of money which is thus every year drawn from Brazil, for the sole purpose of enriching the individual, to whom the salt trade has been farmed out, all the rest of the inhabitants of those countries are made losers; at least their gain is materially prejudiced by the monopoly. The whole commerce of Portugal, indeed, is made to forfeit, by this abuse, infinite emoluments and advantages, which would otherwise accrue to it, from a greater abundance of salt fish, butcher's meat, bacon, cheese, and butter, that would be preserved and brought to market. Thus the royal treasury, for the sake of the comparatively paltry consideration of forty-eight millions of Réis a year, robs itself of much larger sums, which the duties of these products would fetch, but for the factitious dearness of salt.

Unless flesh and fish can be salted or preserved, the marine of Portugal will never attain any great degree of importance; there will never be many cargoes for ships, never many seamen, never a nursery for their instruction. Thus the expense of freight will always be very high; sugar and all other colonial products, will consequently remain very dear; and the colonists will be deprived of a fair competition with foreigners, who will bring the same products to the markets of Portugal, but can afford to sell them cheaper, as they can ship them at a much lower freight. . . .

A single ship, with manufactured goods, from the mother country to Rio Grande, might, for instance, take on board all the wearing apparel, and other articles of luxury, requisite for the inhabitants of those happy plains. But it would be impossible for the same ship to take in at once, and convey from thence the amount of the value of her cargo; either in money -- for there is none at all in those countries, nor can there be any, since there is no commerce -- or in produce, as it would weigh infinitely heavier, and is by far lower, in price, than the goods coming from the mother country. A handkerchief, for instance, is sold for more, at Rio Grande, than a fat ox, and is of no weight at all, compared with the animal.

In order to carry back produce of equal value with the first cargo, the ship from the mother country would be obliged to return to the colonies, twice, or three times, in ballast, consequently with expenses exceeding the returns. The ship would thus always remain debtor, without being able to settle the account, or she would be otherwise forced to place the charges of freight, for two or three voyages, on the goods of a single voyage; which might fairly be said to be pulling up by the roots the commerce of the colonies, and, by the same inference, that of the mother country itself.

On the other hand, such articles might be exported to those colonies, as would equal, as nearly as possible, both in weight and value, the different sorts of colonial produce which would be taken in return. The mother country has, I believe, no article better calculated for this purpose than salt. This alone can make up the cargo of a ship from the mother country, and procure her a freight from the colonies, on her passage home.

If the salt trade to Brazil were once made free, the superabundance of that charming country would no longer be the prey of tigers, and that of its coasts the food of sea monsters. The fisherman, the herdsman, the husbandman, the merchant, would reciprocally lend a helping hand. They would, in concert, supply Portugal with meat, fish, bread, cheese, butter, and other necessaries. This trade would pour millions of additional revenue into the royal coffers. And Portugal would possess a mine of inexhaustible treasure, richer than the mines of Potosí. . . .

Besides the various sorts of wood, useful in building ships, there are in Brazil several others. . . .

But owing to the high price of freight, and the many duties, which must be paid, on the importation of Brazilwood into Portugal, a great part of the value of those noble products are lost to the country from which they are drawn, or they are smuggled into the mother country, or left to spoil in the forests, in which they grow.

With regard to freight, its price must fall, the more commercial navigation increases; but the latter, too, as soon as the laborers are allowed the free sale of their wood, must gain additional vigor, in proportion as the abundance of products is multiplied. On the other hand, if the duties of importation be not taken off, Portugal will not be able to effect anything beneficial in the timber trade, or rather it will become prejudicial to the state, owing to the powerful competition of foreigners in the same branch of commerce.

The dearness of brazilwood, occasioned by these means, in Portugal, will facilitate the importation of foreign timber. This will, of course, give to the revenues of the country a blow doubly severe, by the wilful suppression, in the first place, of the produce of the country, and, in the second, by the money paid for the same articles to foreigners.

Foreign wood not only contains, for the most part, more resin, and is consequently more combustible, and more dangerous in fires, but is also less lasting than that of Brazil. The duties on the importation of this wood should, therefore, be taken off, for the purpose of getting a larger quantity of a commodity, so much better in quality, and so much less dangerous, where fires break out.

The suppression of the duties on all the importation of brazilwood cannot, at all, be deemed a loss to the royal treasury. Those who harbour such an idea, are, to the great prejudice of the public welfare, grossly mistaken.

STRIKING THE CHAINS ON MANUFACTURING (1794)

The hasty departure of the Portuguese royal court from Lisbon for Brazil in 1807 brought a ray of light or a breath of fresh air to the great colony. True, the light was sometimes diluted and the fresh air polluted by ill-considered actions by one or another of the Portuguese emigrés. But, generally speaking, the thirteen years that Dom João remained in Brazil, first as regent and then as king, were a sort of "operation bootstrap" for the colony. One of the first manifestations of the new policy was the decree by the prince regent, less than three months after landing, removing the previous ban on manufacturing in Brazil. The decree is translated by Professor E. Bradford Burns from Pinto de Aguiar, A Abertura dos Portos do Brasil (Bahia: Progresso, 1960).

I, the Prince Regent, make known to one and all: That desiring to promote and further the national wealth, and one of the sources of it being manufacturing and industry which multiply, improve, and give greater value to the provisions and products of Agriculture and the Arts and increase the population by giving work to many laborers and by furnishing means of subsistence to many of My Vassals, who, for lack of such means, would be left to the vices of idleness, and that wishing to remove all obstacles which might diminish or frustrate such advantageous benefits, I am pleased to abolish and revoke all and every prohibition which exists to this respect in the State of Brazil and in My Overseas Domains. Henceforth, it shall be legal for any of My Vassals in any area in which they live to establish any kind of manufacture, without any exception, to make goods in large or small quantities as best suits them. I do therefore annul the Royal Order of January 5, 1785, and any other laws or orders which contradict this decision without making individual and express mention of them. Therefore, I command the President of the Royal Council, Governors, Captains-General, and other Governors of the State of Brazil and of the Overseas Domains and all the Ministers of Justice and other persons to whom knowledge of this is important to carry out and to fulfill this My Royal Order and to disregard those laws which I have hereby revoked and annulled. Given in the Palace of Rio de Janeiro on April 1, 1808.

THE PRINCE.

A ROYAL THRONE (1816)

One of the most politically exalted acts performed by João
as prince regent, in the year before he became King João VI, was
his decree elevating Brazil to equal status with Portugal in the
governance of the empire. In part the action was in response to
a suggestion made by Prince Talleyrand and indirect pressures
from the Congress of Vienna and in part it was a result of João's
fondness for Brazil. The decree was published in Robert Walsh,
Notices of Brazil in 1828 and 1829 (Boston: Richardson, Lord,
and Holbrook, 1831).

D. João, by the Grace of God, Prince Regent of Portugal and the
Algarves, in Africa and Guinea, and of the Conquest, Navigation, and
Commerce of Ethiopia, Arabia, Persia, and India, &c. make known to
those to whom this present Letter of Law shall come, that there being
constantly in my royal mind the most lively desire to cause to prosper
those States which the Divine Providence has confided to my sovereign
rule; and giving, at the same time, its due importance to the magnitude
and locality of my domains in America, to the copiousness and variety
of the precious elements of wealth which it contains; and knowing besides
how advantageous to my faithful subjects in general will be a perfect
union and identity between my kingdom of Portugal, the Algarves, and
my dominions of Brazil, by raising them to that grade and political class,
which, by the aforesaid proposition, they ought to aspire to, and in which
my said dominions have been already considered by the plenipotentiaries
of the powers which form the Congress at Vienna, also in the Treaty of
Alliance concluded on the 8th of April in the current year [1815], as in
the final treaty of the same Congress; I am therefore minded, and it is
my pleasure, to ordain as follows:

1st. That from the publication of this Letter of Law, the State of
Brazil shall be elevated to the dignity, preeminence, and denomination
of the Kingdom of Brazil. 2dly. That my kingdom of Portugal, the Algarves,
and Brazil, shall form from henceforth one only and united kingdom, under
the title of the United Kingdom of Portugal, Brazil, and the Algarves.
3dly. That for the titles inherent in the crown of Portugal, and of which
it has hitherto made use in all its public acts, the new title shall be
substituted of Prince Regent of the United Kingdoms of Portugal, Brazil,
and the Algarves, &c.

Given in the Palace of Rio de Janeiro, the 16th of December, 1815.

THE PRINCE
MARQUES DO AGUIAR.

INDEPENDENCE - AND AN IMPERIAL THRONE (1822)

After the return of King João VI to Portugal the government of that country sought to reduce Brazil to its earlier colonial status. João had foreseen the possible course that events might take and, before leaving Brazil, had counseled his son to cast in his lot with the New World possession if he must make a choice. In the early months of 1822 Pedro, who would soon become Emperor Pedro I, took various steps pointing tentatively toward independence. The climax came on September 7 on the banks of the Ypiranga River near São Paulo. Several of the attendant courtiers described the famous Grito do Ypiranga (Cry of Ypiranga) in letters or diaries. Perhaps the best account was that of Father Belchior Pinheiro de Oliveira, author of the following description translated by Professor E. Bradford Burns from F. Assis Cintra, D. Pedro e o Grito da Independencia (São Paulo: Companhia Melhoramentos, 1921).

The Prince ordered me to read aloud the letters brought by Paulo Bregaro and Antônio Cordeiro. The consisted of the following: an instruction from the Côrtes, a letter from D. João, another from the Princess, another from José Bonifacio and still another from Chamberlain, the secret agent of the Prince. The Côrtes demanded the immediate return of the Prince and the imprisonment and trial of José Bonifacio; the Princess recommended prudence and asked the Prince to listen to the advice of his minister; José Bonifacio told the Prince that he must choose one of two roads to follow: leave immediately for Portugal and make himself the prisoner of the Côrtes, as was the situation of D. João VI, or remain and proclaim the independence of Brazil becoming either its Emperor or King; Chamberlain gave information that the party of D. Miguel, in Portugal, was victorious and that they spoke openly of the disinheritance of D. Pedro in favor of D. Miguel; D. João advised his son to obey the Portuguese law. D. Pedro, trembling with rage, grabbed the letters from my hands and crumpling them up threw them on the ground and stomped on them. He left them lying there, but I picked them up and kept them. Then, after buttoning up and arranging his uniform (he had just been to the edge of the stream of Ypiranga agonized by a painful attack of dysentery), he turned toward me and asked: "What now, Father Belchior?"

I quickly responded, "If your Highness does not declare himself King of Brazil, you will be made a prisoner of the Côrtes and perhaps disinherited by them. The only course is independence and separation."

Accompanied by me, Cordeiro, Bregaro, Carlota, and others, D. Pedro silently walked toward our horses at the side of the road. Suddenly he halted in the middle of the road and said to me, "Father Belchior, they asked for it and they will get it. The Côrtes is persecuting me and calling me an adolescent and a Brazilian. Well, now let them see their adolescent in action. From today on our relations with them are finished.

I want nothing more from the Portuguese government, and I proclaim Brazil forevermore separated from Portugal."

With enthusiasm we immediately answered, "Long live liberty!" Long live an independent Brazil! Long live D. Pedro!"

The Prince turned to his adjutant and said, "Tell my guard that I have just declared the complete independence of Brazil. We are free from Portugal."

Lieutenant Canto e Melo rode toward a market where most of the soldiers of the guard remained. He returned to the Prince with them shouting enthusiastically in favor of an independent and separate Brazil, D. Pedro, and the Catholic Religion.

D. Pedro before the guard said, "The Portuguese Côrtes wants to enslave and to persecute us. Henceforth our relations are broken. Not one tie unites us!" And tearing from his hat the blue and white emblem decreed by the Côrtes as the symbol of the Portuguese nation, he threw it on the ground, saying, "Throw away that symbol, soldiers! Long live independence, liberty, and the separation of Brazil!"

We responded with a shout in favor of an independent and separate Brazil and another for D. Pedro.

The Prince unsheathed his sword, and the civilians removed their hats. D. Pedro said, "By my blood, by my honor, and with God's help, I swear to liberate Brazil."

"We all swear to it," shouted the rest.

D. Pedro sheathed his sword, an act repeated by the guard, went to the head of the crowd, turned, and rose up in the stirrups to cry, "Brazilians, our motto from this day forward will be 'Independence or Death.' "

Seated firmly in his saddle, he spurred his handsome horse and galloped, followed by his retinue, toward São Paulo, where he was lodged by Brigadier Jordão, Captain Antônio Silva Prado, and others, who worked miracles in order to cheer up the prince.

After dismounting, D. Pedro ordered his adjutant to go at once to the goldsmith Lessa and have made a small disk in gold bearing the words "Independence or Death" to be fastened on the arm with ribbons of green and gold.

Wearing the emblem he appeared at the theatre where my dear friends Alfêres Aquins and Father Ildefonso acclaimed him the King of Brazil.

Throughout the theatre were yellow and green ribbons. They hung from the walls, from the boxes, from the arms of the men and from the hair and dresses of the women.

REPUBLICANISM SHAKES THE THRONE (1870)

The catalyst of the Paraguayan War (1864-70) speeded a number of changes in Brazilian life: growing ambitions on the part of the army officer group, an intensification of friction between the government and the Church, an increasing sentiment for supplanting imperial by republican government, expanding dissatisfaction with slavery, among others. There were, of course, other factors involved; abolition of slavery in the United States was naturally significantly related to sentiment for such action in Brazil.

Intellectual ferment in Brazilian life was stimulated by the impact of European positivist philosophy, especially as expounded by the French writer Auguste Comte. The influence of Comtian positivism was felt not only in Brazil but in a number of Spanish American countries as well. Comtian doctrines were especially attractive to a coterie of army officers and one of them, Col. Benjamin Constant, was led thereby to become the chief advocate of republican government. A new Republican Party published its Republican Manifesto on December 3, 1870. This document became a focus for the growing republican sentiment in Brazil, a sentiment which would be triumphant within less than two decades.

The following excerpts from the Republican Manifesto were translated by Professor E. Bradford Burns from Djacir Menezes (ed.), O Brasil no Pensamento Brasileiro (Rio de Janeiro: Ministerio da Educação e Cultura, 1957).

In this country, which considers itself constitutional and where only delegated, responsible powers should be able to act, it happens, because of a defect in the system, that there is only one active, omnipotent, perpetual power, superior to the law and to public opinion, and it is, of course, the sacred power, inviolable and irresponsible.

Privilege invades all aspects of society -- in synthesis, it is the fabric of our society and politics -- privilege of religion, privilege of race, privilege of intellect, privilege of position, which constitutes all the arbitrary and hateful distinctions that create in the bosom of civil and political society and the monstrous superiority of one over all or of a few over the many.

Our country owes its moral decadence, administrative disorganization, and economic disturbances, which threaten to devour the future after ruining the present, to the disequilibrium of forces, to that atrophying pressure.

Despite a half century of existence as an independent national community, Brazilian society finds itself today facing the problem of its political organization as if it had just now emerged from colonial chaos. . . .

A Chamber of Deputies subject to dissolution at the will of the sovereign and a life-term Senate selected by the sovereign in no way can constitute the legitimate representation of the country.

Liberty of conscience nullified by a privileged Church; economic freedom suppressed by restrictive legislation; liberty of the press subordinated to the jurisdiction of the functionaries of the Government; freedom of association dependent on the pleasure of the authorities; freedom of instruction infringed upon by arbitrary governmental inspection and by official monopoly; individual freedom subject to preventative imprisonment, to recruitment, to the discipline of the national guard, deprived of the full guarantee of habeas corpus; these are the conditions under the present system of government.

A sovereign, perpetual, and irresponsible power creates with a nod of the head the executive by selecting the ministers, the legislature by choosing the Senators and designating the Deputies, and the judiciary by naming the judges.

Such is in essence the political mechanism of the Constitution of 1824; such are the sophisms by means of which the Emperor reigns, rules and regulates. . . .

In Brazil the desire to establish federalism takes precedence even over the democratic idea. The topography of our territory, the diverse zones into which it is divided, the various climates and the different products, the mountains and the rivers indicate the necessity of modeling administration and local government to accompany and to respect the very divisions created by nature and imposed by the immensity of our territory. . . .

From 1824 to 1848, from the Federation of the Equator to the Revolution of Pernambuco, one can say that the electric current which passed through the Provinces shaking the social organism came from a single source -- the desire for local independence, the idea of federation, the sentiment for provincial autonomy. . . .

Provincial autonomy is for us Republicans ... a cardinal and solemn principle which we inscribe on our banner.

Federalism based on the reciprocal independence of the Provinces, elevated to the category of States, linked only by the bond of the same nationality and by the solidarity of the great interests of representation and defense is what we adopt in our program as being the only means capable of maintaining the community of the Brazilian family. . . .

National sovereignty can only exist, can only be recognized and practiced in a nation whose parliament, elected by the participation of all the citizens, has the supreme direction and pronounces the final word in public business.

If there exists, in any constitution, an element of compulsion to the principle of democratic liberty, the national sovereignty is violated, it is null, incapable of the salutary effects of the modern formula of government -- the government of all for all.

Another indispensable condition of national sovereignty is that it is inalienable and that only exercise of it can be delegated. . . .

From this principle it follows that when the people cede a part of their sovereignty they do so to create not a master but a servant, that is, a functionary.

The consequence of this is that the functionary has to be revocable, mobile, elective, the very essence of the formula of the modern state -- the mobility of persons and the perpetuity of function -- opposed to which are the systems, such as the one ruling over us, exalting heredity, inviolability, irresponsibility. . . .

Strengthened by our right and by our conscience, we present ourselves before our fellow citizens resolutely waving the banner of the Federal Republican Party.

We are from America and we desire to be Americans.

Our monarchical form of government is in its essence and practice contrary and hostile to the right and to the interests of the American States.

The continuance of that form will be, in addition to the origin of oppression in the interior, the perpetual source of hostility and war with our neighbors.

To Europe we pass as a democratic monarchy which neither inspires sympathy nor provokes adhesion. To America we pass as a monarchical democracy where the instinct and force of the people cannot predominate over the will and omnipotence of the sovereign.

Under such consitions, Brazil can consider itself an isolated nation, not only in the Americas but in the world.

We direct our efforts to end this situation by putting ourselves in fraternal contact with all peoples and in democratic solidarity with the continent of which we are a part.

THE LAW OF THE FREE WOMB (1871)

Brazil did not have to fight a civil war, as did the United States, to rid itself of the institution of slavery. Instead, the disappearance of such bondage came piecemeal, by legislation and other actions, in the second half of the nineteenth century. One of the most notable laws bearing on the problem was the so-called Law of the Free Womb, dated September 28, 1871. Its effect was to make free all children born to slaves after its promulgation. The law was sanctioned by the princess regent, an ardent opponent of slavery, during an absence of her father, the emperor, from Brazil. It also fell to the lot of Princess Isabel, again acting as regent on May 13, 1888, to sanction the law definitively abolishing slavery in Brazil.

This translation of the Law of the Free Womb is taken from British and Foreign State Papers, 1871-1872 (London: William Ridgway, 1877).

The Princess Imperial, Regent, in the name of His Majesty the Emperor Senhor D. Pedro II, makes known to all the subjects of the Empire, that the General Assembly has decreed, and that she has sanctioned, the following Law:

Art. I. The children of women slaves that may be born in the Empire from the date of this Law shall be considered to be free.

Sec. 1. The said minors shall remain with and be under the dominion of the owners of the mother, who shall be obliged to rear and take care of them until such children shall have completed the age of eight years.

On the child of the slave attaining this age, the owner of its mother shall have the option either of receiving from the State the indemnification of 600 dollars, or of making use of the services of the minor until he shall have completed the age of twenty-one years.

In the former event the Government will receive the minor, and will dispose of him in conformity with the provisions of the present Law.

The pecuniary indemnification above fixed shall be paid in Government bonds, bearing interest at six per cent. per annum, which will be considered extinct at the end of thirty years.

The declaration of the owner must be made within thirty days, counting from the day on which the minor shall complete the age of eight years; and should he not do so within that time it will be understood that he embraces the option of making use of the service of the minor.

Sec. 2. Any one of those minors may ransom himself from the onus of servitude, by means of a previous pecuniary indemnification, offered by himself, or by any other person, to the owner of his mother, calculating the value of his services for the time which shall still remain unexpired to complete the period, should there be no agreement on the quantum of the said indemnification.

Sec. 3. It is also incumbent on owners to rear and bring up the children which the daughters of their female slaves may have while they are serving the same owners.

Such obligation, however, will cease as soon as the service of the mother ceases. Should the latter die within the term of servitude the children may be placed at the disposal of the Government.

Sec. 4. Should the female slave obtain her freedom, her children under eight years of age who may be under the dominion of her owners shall, by virtue of Sec. 1, be delivered up, unless she shall prefer leaving them with him, and he consents to their remaining.

Sec. 5. In case of the female slave being made over to another owner her free children under twelve years of age shall accompany her, the new owner of the said slave being invested with the rights and obligations of his predecessor.

Sec. 6. The services of the children of female slaves shall cease to be rendered before the term marked in Sec. 1, if by decision of the Criminal Judge it be known that the owner of the mothers ill-treat the children, inflicting on them severe punishments.

Sec. 7. The right conferred on owners by Sec. 1 shall be transferred in cases of direct succession; the child of a slave must render his services to the person to whose share in the division of property the said slave shall belong.

II. The Government may deliver over to associations which they shall have authorized, the children of the slaves that may be born from the date of this Law forward, and given up or abandoned by the owners of said slaves, or taken away from them by virtue of Article I, Sec. 6.

Sec. 1. The said associations shall have a right to the gratuitous services of the minors, until they shall have completed the age of twenty-one years, and may hire out their services, but shall be bound --

1st. To rear and take care of the said minors.

2ndly. To save a sum for each of them, out of the amount of wages, which for this purpose is reserved in the respective statutes.

3rdly. To seek to place them in a proper situation when their term of service shall be ended.

Sec. 2. The associations referred to in the previous paragraph shall be subject to the inspection of Judges of the Orphans' Court, in as far as affects minors.

Sec. 3. The disposition of this Article is applicable to foundling asylums, and to the persons whom the Judges of the Orphans' Court charge with the education of the said minors, in default of associations or houses established for that purpose.

Sec. 4. The Government has the free right of ordering the said minors to be taken into the public establishments, the obligations imposed by Sec. 1 on the authorised associations being in this case transferred to the State.

III. As many slaves as correspond in value to the annual disposable sum from the emancipation fund shall be freed in each province of the Empire.

Sec. 1. The emancipation fund arises from --

1st. The tax on slaves.

2ndly. General tax on transfer of the slaves as property.

3rdly. The proceeds of six lotteries per annum, free of tax, and the tenth part of those which may be granted from this time forth, to be drawn in the capital of the Empire.

4thly. The fines imposed by virtue of this Law.

5thly. The sums which may be marked in the general budget, and in those of the provinces and municipalities.

6thly. Subscriptions, endowments, and legacies for that purpose.

Sec. 2. The sums marked in the provincial and municipal budgets, as also the subscriptions, endowments, and legacies for the local purpose, shall be applied for the manumission of slaves in the provinces, districts, municipalities, and parishes designated.

IV. The slave is permitted to form a saving fund from what may come to him through gifts, legacies, and inheritances, and from what, by consent of his owner, he may obtain by his labor and economy. The Government will see to the regulations as to the placing and security of said savings.

Sec. 1. By the death of the slave half of his savings shall belong to his surviving widow, if there be such, and the other half shall be transmitted to his heirs in conformity with civil law.

In default of heirs the savings shall be adjudged to the emancipation fund of which Article III treats.

Sec. 2. The slave who, through his savings, may obtain means to pay his value has a right to freedom.

If the indemnification be not fixed by agreement it shall be settled by arbitration. In judicial sales or inventories the price of manumission shall be that of the valuation.

Sec. 3. It is further permitted the slave, in furtherance of his liberty, to contract with a third party the hire of his future services, for a term not exceeding seven years, by obtaining the consent of his master, and approval of the Judge of the Orphans' Court.

Sec. 4. The slave that belongs to joint proprietors, and is freed by one of them, shall have a right to his freedom by indemnifying the other owners with the share of the amount which belongs to them. This idemnification may be paid by services rendered for a term not exceeding seven years, in conformity with the preceding paragraph.

Sec. 5. The manumission, with the clause of services during a certain time, shall not become annulled by want of fulfilling the said clause, but the freed man shall be compelled to fulfil, by means of labour in the public establishments, or by contracting for his services with private persons.

Sec. 6. Manumissions, whether gratuitous or by means of onus, shall be exempted from all duties, emoluments, or expenses.

Sec. 7. In any case of alienation or transfer of slaves, the separation of husband and wife, and children under twelve years of age from father or mother, is prohibited under penalty of annulment.

Sec. 8. If the division of property among heirs or partners does not permit the union of a family, and none of them prefers remaining with the family by replacing the amount of the share belonging to the other interested parties, the said family shall be sold and the proceeds shall be divided among the heirs.

Sec. 9. The ordination, Book 4th, title 63, in the part which revokes freedom on account of ingratitude, is set aside.

V. The Emancipation Societies which are formed, and those which may for the future be formed, shall be subject to the inspection of the Judges of the Orphans' Court.

Sole paragraph. The said societies shall have the privilege of commanding the services of the slaves whom they may have liberated, to indemnify themselves for the sum spent in their purchase.

VI. The following shall be declared free:

Sec. 1. The slaves belonging to the State, the Government giving them such employment as they may deem fit.

Sec. 2. The slave given in usufruct to the Crown.

Sec. 3. The slaves of unclaimed inheritances.

Sec. 4. The slaves who have been abandoned by their owners.

Should these have abandoned the slaves from the latter being invalids they shall be obliged to maintain them, except in case of their own penury, the maintenance being charged by the Judge of the Orphans' Court.

Sec. 5. In general the slaves liberated by virtue of this Law shall be under the inspection of Government during five years. They will be obliged to hire themselves under pain of compulsion; if they lead an idle life they shall be made to work in the public establishments.

The compulsory labour, however, shall cease so soon as the freed man shall exhibit an engagement of hire.

VII. In trials in favour of freedom --

Sec. 1. The process shall be summary.

Sec. 2. There shall be appeal ex officio when the decisions shall be against the freedom.

VIII. The Government will order the special registration of all the slaves existing in the Empire to be proceeded with, containing a declaration of name, sex, age, state, aptitude for work, and filiation of each, if such should be known.

Sec. 1. The date on which the registry ought to commence closing shall be announced beforehand, the longest time possible being given for preparation by means of edicts repeated, in which shall be inserted the dispositions of the following paragraph.

Sec. 2. The slaves who, through the fault or omission of the parties interested, shall not have been registered up to one year after the closing of the register, shall, de facto, be considered as free.

Sec. 3. For registering each slave the owner shall pay, once only, the emolument of 500 réis, if done within the term marked, and one dollar should that be exceeded. The produce of those emoluments shall go towards the expenses of registering, and the surplus to the emancipation fund.

Sec. 4. The children of a slave mother, who by this Law became free, shall also be registered in a separate book.

Those persons who have become remiss shall incur a fine of 100 dollars to 200 dollars, repeated as many times as there may be individuals omitted: and for fraud, in the penalties of Article CLXXIX of the Criminal Code.

Sec. 5. The parish priests shall be obliged to have special books for the registry of births and deaths of the children of slaves born from and after the date of this law. Each omission will subject the parish priest to a fine of 100 dollars.

IX. The Government, in its regulations, can impose fines of as much as 100 dollars, and the penalty of imprisonment up to one month.

X. All contrary dispositions are revoked.

Therefore, order all authorities to whom, &c. Given at the Palace of Rio de Janeiro, on the 28th September, 1871. 50th of the Independence and of the Empire.

PRINCESS IMPERIAL, REGENT.

THEODORO MACHADO FREIRE PEREIRA DA SILVA.

DROUGHT -- THE SCOURGE OF THE NORTHEAST (1878)

Climatic conditions in the Brazilian northeast, especially in the state of Ceará, have perennially posed a problem of extremely serious proportions. The area has been subject from the earliest time to recurrent droughts which have brought their inevitable aftermaths of malnutrition and starvation, disease, economic dislocation, mass migrations from the area, and other grave consequences. It was in recognition of the problem that the constitution of 1946 included in Article 198 the following provision: "The Union [the federal government] shall expend, annually, upon works and services of social and economic assistance for the execution of the defense plans against the effects of the so-called drought of the Northeast, an amount never inferior to three percent of all revenue." It was also in recognition of the impact of the droughts that Francisco Julião in the 1950s and 1960s made the northeast the scene of his activity in organizing "Peasant Leagues" to try to right the sufferings of the lower rural classes by political action. Julião said, "I have a general on my side -- Hunger."

A particularly serious drought occurred in 1877-79. A naturalist from the United States, Herbert H. Smith, saw at first hand some of its effects and recorded them in his book, Brazil, the Amazons and the Coast (London: Sampson, Low 1880), from which the following extracts are taken.

My personal observations of this great calamity were confined to a part of December, 1878. I reached Fortaleza on the 19th of that month, when the deathrate from small-pox had gone down to about 350 per day. Aided by His Excellency, President Julip, and by Sr. Morsing, I was able, during the ten days of my stay, to make careful observations, both at Fortaleza and in the interior. It was not a pleasant subject; but as the facts I gleaned may have some historical value, I will epitomize them here.

At first I saw very few signs of the pestilence. The city streets were clean and neat; here and there I noticed refugees standing idly by the street corners, and some of these had small-pox scars on their faces. About the public storehouses there were carts and porters carrying provisions; no signs of starvation were apparent, for the people had been well fed since May.

I stopped to engage a room at the little hotel; the landlord, after some questioning, acknowledged that there were two small-pox cases in the house; but added, truly enough, that no better place could be found; the sick here were carefully isolated, and well cared for.

I was much impressed with the apparent indifference of the people to their danger. The pestilence was, indeed, a universal subject of conversation, but everybody seemed to rest in an easy fatalism or blindness;

speaking of the daily death-rate as one tells of the killed and wounded in a battle -- a real event, but far away. I did not hear of a single resident who left the town on account of the danger; there was the usual amount of dissipation and flirtation; the market square was crowded, and men drove hard bargains; in outward appearance the little city had hardly changed since 1876.

Later in the day, I walked out to the refugee camps on the southern side of the city. The huts were wretched beyond description; many were built of boughs, or of poles, covered with an imperfect thatch of palm-leaves, and patched up with bits of boards and rags. Here whole families were croweded together in narrow spaces; filthy, as only these Ceará Arabs can be; ragged, unkempt, lounging on the sands, a fit prey for disease. No measure had been taken to cleanse the camp; the ground, in many places, was covered with fiflth and refuse; water, obtained from a pool near by, was unfit to drink. If the pestilence was hidden in the city, it was visible everywhere in the camps. Half-recovered patients sat apart, but scarcely healed; in almost every hut the sick were lying, horrible with the foul disease. Many dead were waiting for the body carriers; many more would be waiting at the morning round. Yet here, among the sick and dying and dead, there was the same indifference to danger that I had noticed in the city. The peasants were talking and laughing with each other; three or four were gathered about a mat, gambling for biscuits; everywhere the ghastly patients and ghastlier corpses were passed unnoticed; they were too common to objects of curiosity.

Most of these people had come from the interior with the great exodus, and they had been fed by the Government for eight or nine months. As easily managed as children, they were, like children, fractious and careless, and improvident. From the first, they should have been placed under rigid military discipline; with the guidance of competent persons, they should have been made to construct good houses, arrange the streets and sections, for their better government; cleanliness of body and surroundings should have been enforced under the severest penalties; and every able-bodied man and woman should have been employed in work of some kind. But Brazilians everywhere are neglectful of sanitary measures; witness the dirty, badly-drained Rio streets, where yellow fever walks unstayed; witness the epidemic that ran through the army during the Paraguayan war, carrying off far more than the enemy's bullets.

In the morning I walked farther away from the city, where the strips of woodland were as bare as a winter landscape at home, and only a few mandioc fields escaped the general ruin. Here and there I passed lonely huts. Once I stopped to ask for a drink of water, but the woman who was sitting before the door told me that she had none, for the nearest pool was half a mile away, and she was sick and could not fill the calabash. No doubt her story was true, for her face was scarlet with fever, and she complained of a throbbing headache, constant symptom of the dreaded disease. Within the hut were three children; one, like the mother, was suffering with fever and headache; another was covered with small-pox pustules; the third child, a baby, was just dying. A man who was passing brought some water to the hut. I suppose that the woman and children were carried to the lazaretto on the following morning, but among so many patients they could receive little care. The three hospitals were overcrowded, and the new patients could only come in as the daily deaths and few recoveries left the cots vacant.

There was a cemetary near the town, where the dead were buried decently, in separate graves. But this was the city ground, from which bodies of those who had died of small-pox were generally excluded. Two miles west of the city, a much larger ground received the pestilence dead. Every morning searchers examined the huts, and carried away the bodies; as they were not allowed to take their burdens through the streets, the carried them around, either on the southern side, by a little-used path, or along the beach. At sunrise, when I went to bathe in the surf, a constant procession of those body carriers was passing. Sometimes the dead were wrapped in hammocks and slung to poles; oftener they were simply tied to the pole, two or three, perhaps, together, and so borne by two or four carriers; child corpses were thrown into shallow trays which were carried on men's heads. By eight o'clock the stream had lessened; but all through the day the ghastly sight was repeated at intervals. People who lived near the beach became accustomed to this constant funeral, and gave little heed to it.

At the Lagoa Funda ground the dead were buried in trenches, twelve together; "Unless," said one of the overseers, "they come too fast for the diggers; then we put fifteen or twenty in, conforme." The man had been here so long that he regarded the bodies as so many logs. For myself, I was not yet educated to this point; sick and faint, I turned away from the horrible trench and the fetid air. The bodies were buried deep but under loose sand; two thousand of these trenches were poisoning the air, and the stench was almost unbearable. It is recorded of the London plague that men died in the pits they were digging; here the workmen had fallen dead, not from the disease, but from asphyxia, the result of foul air; this happened only where a new trench was dug near an old one. It was very difficult to obtain men for this service, and no wonder.

One of the largest lazarettos was close by the gate of this cemetery; indeed, all the bodies had to pass between two of the buildings, and through the open windows the patients could look out upon the endless procession. I suppose that they were too ill to heed it, but to the poor sertanejo [an inhabitant of the parched interior area] who saw his friend brought here, the hospital must have been almost identified with the cemetery. I was told that ninety per cent of the patients died, and it was a matter of convenience to have the burial-place so near.

At this time the hospitals were of little value, for they could not contain the thirty thousand sick, and the wards were so overcrowded that the patients received less care than they would have in their own huts. It seems probable to me that, in a place so thoroughly infected, slight cases may have been aggravated by fresh poison, until the mortality was greatly increased. Be this as it may, the death-rate was very high here, and the disease assumed its worst forms.

As in many other epidemics the mortality was greatest among strong, vigorous men; children often escaped. I was told of one merchant who had twenty-four workmen in his employ; of these, seventeen died during November and December. Another man had nine clerks in his office, of whom he lost six within two weeks. Whole households were swept away. In many of the richer families, the ladies were driven to the menial services, because their servants had died, and it was impossible to obtain new ones. Vaccination was not always a complete preventive, but it invariably served to check the violence of the disease, so that the patient generally recovered. It was reported -- with what truth I do not know -- that men had been known to have the small-pox twice within a few months; in this case the second attack was very slight.

When the small-pox scourge was at its height, a strange and terrible disease appeared at Fortaleza; by some this was supposed to be a new epidemic, and there were fearful whispers of black plague. It is probable, however, that this was an aggravated form of small-pox; it was characterized by the appearance of black spots on the body, and I believe that the cases were invariably fatal, even before the pustules appeared. About the end of December, the wife of the provincial president was attacked with this "black small-pox" and died within two days.

Amid all this suffering the people celebrated the Christmas festival, with music and feasting and rejoicing. Of the two thousand men and women who knelt in the church, probably many were infected, but no one seemed to fear the contact of a neighbor. Before the service, some who were dying were brought in hammocks to the church-door, to be confessed.

I believe that the priests of Fortaleza did their duty well, all through the pestilence. There were, indeed, no funeral services and few ante-mortem confessions; the death-harvest was too great. But I often saw the younger priests visiting the worst infected camps, not with attendants and gorgeous trappings, but alone, doing their work as the old missionaries did, in the face of danger.

At Pacatuba I found the state of affairs even worse than at Fortaleza. More than half the inhabitants were stricken, and the daily death-rate was frightful. Here, crawling about the railroad station and begging, were diseased children; here, at the house where I stopped, the servants were convalescent patients. I visited many huts in succession, and in each there were from one to five sick.

From this point, almost to Baturité, I rode along the line of the new railroad, where thousands of workmen were employed. Here the change was as agreeable as it was great. The workmen and their families were domicilied in good barracks, and the sick were rigidly isolated; sanitary rules were enforced to some extent. Vaccination had been introduced, and no well man was permitted to be idle. Under these circumstances, I found a steady improvement as I advanced, until I felt that I had left the pestilence and its horrors behind me. Then indeed the ride became a delightful one. Along the hill-sides there had been a few showers, and the trees, which had been bare for eighteen months, began to put out a few timid buds. At Baturité there was running water, for the springs had held out even through two years of drought; here the hill-sides, in many places, were fresh and green, with bright plantations and tangled forests; it was an oasis in the wilderness.

THE SPECTER OF MILITARISM (1910)

Militarism is a flower (weed?) of relatively late growth in Brazil. The peacful attainment of independence in 1822 precluded the early development of a military organization, atmosphere, or psychology of significance. The half-century reign of Dom Pedro II might have contributed continuously to the growth and dominance of civilism had it not been for the ugly fact of the Paraguayan War. This conflict (1864-70) inevitably increased the size and enhanced the importance of the army. Key participation by a number of army officers, notably Col. Constant, in the agitation for a republic widened the gap between the army and the emperor, who was a pronounced pacifist.

Establishment of the republic in 1889 was essentially the result of a military coup and the initial provisional government was in effect an army junta led by the inept Marshal Deodoro da Fonseca. Civilian rule was restored in 1894, but by 1910 maneuvering to return one of the military to the presidency was again taking place. The candidate of the army was Marshal Hermes da Fonseca, the equally inept nephew of the first president. Opposing him was Ruy Barbosa, the principal author of the constitution of 1891, an articulate spokesman of civilian control of the government, and a consistent and persistent enemy of militarism.

Democracy by 1910 was but lightly rooted in Brazil. State loyalties tended to take precedence over any national patriotism. Political parties on a countrywide basis were almost nonexistent, though Barbosa tried to organize a Civilista party -- which promptly disintegrated after he lost the manipulated election.

Though Barbosa was virtually foreordained to lose the controlled election, he made a valiant campaign against militarism. That phenomenon, and military participation in politics, would become more frequent in the future, and since 1964 have been ever-present facts of life in Brazil. Barbosa's was an early voice against them. The following passages from his 1910 campaign speeches are translated by E. Bradford Burns in E. Bradford Burns (editor), A Documentary History of Brazil (New York: Alfred A. Knopf, Inc., 1966). ©1966 by E. Bradford Burns. Reprinted by permission.

The Republic was the undeniable solution. But the dilettantism with which public sentiment received it threatened its existence from the beginning with incalculable dangers. An organism without reactions, our democracy naturally delivered itself to the instruments of force. The nation continued to sleep in its habits of a former day, when a system of government less accessible to the rule of ambitions had succeeded in conciliating with a relative tranquility.

Under a more delicate and complex constitution, popular lack of resistance was the open door to inordinate factionalism. As long as the nation did not take hold of itself, we were destined to be, in crisis after crisis, the humble and unprotected victim of the reappearances of our native vice. From 1889 to 1909 there was not one national movement: all were military movements. Who, on November 23, deposed the first president? Who, immediately thereafter, in one State after another controlled and ran the governments and local justice? In 1892, who composed the exposed April conspiracy and who crushed it with an arbitrary blow of unconstitutional retirements, exonerations, and exiles? Who rebelled in 1893 and 1894 against the constituted government? Who, in 1897, crowned the expedition of Canudos with an assassination attempt on President Prudente de Morais? In 1901 who took President Campos Sales by surprise and induced him to imprison an admiral? Who, in 1904, during the Rodrigues Alves administration, went out into the streets of the capital with gun in hand and with a banner of insurrections unfurled against the Chief of State? Who, this year [1910], during the administration of Afonso Pena, carried to the Palace of Catête the rumors of a candidate supported by the will of the armed forces?

These are the spasms of a periodical illness which at more or less brief intervals break national apathy. These seizures occur intermittenly in each presidency so that none escapes his share of a violent crisis. And a circumstance at first glance contradictory, but on closer examination related to the character of the illness, is the fact that the military presidents are the ones most disturbed by the militaristic explosions. During the first [military presidency], the government itself caused the disturbance by a coup de'etat the Marshal directed against Congress. During the second, the disturbance came from the armed forces in the form of a nearly victorious revolt against the government of a general. This helps to point out that military institutions and militaristic vices, far from blending together, oppose and destroy each other just as the organic injuries destroy the organs they afflict. Before offending civil laws, militarism attacks the core of military laws. It begins by affronting them in their essence, the subordination of armed force to civil order, in order to undermine them later in their express canons, where each one of those outrages has a severe penalty which should be applied against it.

Between military institutions and militarism there is, in substance, an abyss of radical contradiction. Militarism, government of the nation by the sword, ruins the military institutions, the legal subordination of the sword to the nation. The military institutions juridically organize force. Militarism disorganizes it. Militarism is to the army what fanaticism is to religion, what charlatanry is to science, what industrialism is to industry, what merchantilism is to commerce, what Caesarism it to royalty, what demagogy is to democracy, what absolutism is to order, what egoism is to the ego. [The military institutions] are order; [militarism] is anarchy. They, morality; it, corruption. They, national defense; it, the dismantling, the erosion, the crumbling of that defense, more expensive in the budgets but reduced in its real effectiveness to a sham.

In its present manifestation, ladies and gentlemen, our republican illness assumed a dissembling form which permits the partisans of the candidacy of the marshal the duplicity of publicly denying a militaristic tendency, which is confessed, sustained, flaunted, first in secret and with mystery, then with intrepidity and with threats from lip to lip, ear to ear, group to group. Previous presidents had suffered the attack under the form of conspiracies or of uprisings. The last one received the crafty, explosive artifact wrapped in the guise of a ministerial candidate [for president]. Against the candidacy of a civilian minister, put forth, as one would suppose, by the Chief of State, was raised, sustained with a scowl of force, the candidacy of the military minister. This head of Medusa, the political-military men imagined, ought to frighten the president and cause him to abandon hastily the candidacy of [David] Campista. Given to this allurement, the adversaries of this [candidacy of Campista] would not refuse, in exchange for their apparent victory over the presidential will, the role of the responsible party for the candidacy which they had dictated under a dilemma, the other of whose alternatives was "rebellion in the streets."

This idea [of the candidacy of Marshal Hermes da Fonseca] had been held for a long time. João Pinheiro had notice of it in February of 1908. During the excursion of the Minister of War [Hermes da Fonseca] to Berlin, there circulated timorous news of it. Later, in preparation for it there was discussion of a military manifesto to be written here but to be made public anonymously in the military districts of the North. Thus, with the Campista candidacy upset because of the retreat from the situation in Minas Gerais, the fatal thought to run [Hermes da Fonseca] had been matured through long days of incubation.

The civilian politicians knew it. More than once I heard from those political leaders, the most prominent ones today in the military campaign, expressions of horror at the possibility of "calamity" and others which emphasized "a regression of fifteen years in republican experience."

But the military politicians did not count in vain on the selfishness, cowardice, and ambition of the civilian politicians. Weakness, emotion, and personal calculation did their work. Hence, the current of opinion which expresses the rights of the country to the choice of the Chief of State formed against the nomination of the civilian minister, and in the name of those same rights leads today, gaily decked in bunting, to the nomination of the Minister of War. Well, is is not clear that those in opposition to the candidacy of Campista wanted nothing else? The monster was the candidate of Catête [Presidential Palace]. To the candidate of the barracks there would be no objection. The national candidate was found. It remained only to consecrate him with national approval, national satisfaction, and the national anthem. Let the press, oratory, and banquets do their work now and the miracle will be brought about. Now there you have it: the sword wrapped in the Constitution.

·   ·   ·

"They will have to swallow it." We will have to swallow it for good or for bad is the consecrated phrase, the last argument of that attack on the nation. We have not accustomed [this nation] to fight. Its political traditions are weak. Its republican habits are neglected. Its democracy is composed of humiliations, deceptions, and abdications. Now, in our time, militarism invaded it, corrupted it, mutilated it. The disease has left the organism in a sad condition. In such a state the conspirators count on our regression to a military epoch. Republicans who in the last days of Floriano [Peixoto] had prevented the declaration of dictatorship with a decided non possumus today enlist in its service. Once this is accomplished, Brazil will plunge forever into the servitude of the armed forces, continuous or remittent, periodic or uninterrupted, manifest or disguised, but eternal, organic, incurable.

From all this results a situation on which our entire future depends. In order to solve it and to avoid catastrophe it will be necessary to excite the nation, all of it, the moral forces of the country, the cooperation of all shades of opinion, moderate or radical, liberal or conservative, unbelieving or believing, all of Brazil, exactly as when a foreign enemy menaces the fatherland. Because, like the foreign enemy, militarism is the common scourge of all opinions, all interests, all national rights: the extortion of liberty, the obliteration of intelligence, the prohibition of civic pride, the destruction of credit, the negation of constitutional government, the empire of master without law, responsibility, culture, redress, or hope.

What greater program could there be than one of preventing that collapse of our system of government? Before organizing the nation into parties, it is urgent to save it. We will recapture its strength in civic order, and, in the open field of that victory, which we will have won, with dedication, competence, energy, we will then opportunely undertake an examination of the necessary reforms. Even the most impatient will not have to wait long if the nation is with us in the battle on March 1st. If that battle be lost, as it will be if we do not carry the struggle to the level of the general public, God knows how long the supporters of the party system will have to cherish their hopes. But now, in the imminence of the fight, while the invasion beats against the walls of the city and the insistent shouts of enemy bravura shock us, to defend fundamental conclusions about the organization of parties and the elaboration of political creeds could only be done by rebelling against common sense.

This matter of party platforms at this moment is beginning to take on characteristics of a morbid epidemic or a ridiculous marotte. Back in the period of historical republicanism one understands the zeal for a platform. I do not wish bad luck to those professions of individual or collective faith. Then I believed in them more than I now believe in them. Like others, I paid tribute to superstition because there is no spirit or age that does not have its weakness. But what really sounds to me like a carnival jest is the distribution of platforms of the civilian and military candidates carried out by the enthusiasts of the May Convention.

My platform according to them, only can be revisionism. The platform of the Marshal is the Constitution. There is talk of another which is in the making, but that one is accessory to this other one, the principal idea, the maximum program, the supreme core: to maintain the Constitution, to defend it, to exalt it, to guard it. Now, this poor Constitution, the besmirched lady of so many slights, is going to meet, at last, with her knight errant.

I will leave for another time the task of outlining my platform, the question of my duties toward the revisionism. Everything cannot fit into one speech. For today, to conclude, I will stick to the question of the Constitution between the two candidates.

It is extraordinary how God writes the law in crooked lines. The government of the first marshal [Deodoro da Fonseca] tried to place over the Constitution his own dictatorship by dissolving Congress. The government of the second marshal [Floriano Peixoto] sought to consolidate its dictatorship over that Constitution by the postponement of Congress. The government of the third marshal [Hermes da Fonseca] would come, by acclamation of Congress, to save the Constitution from dictatorships.

In the singular discernment of this choice, what above all things makes me marvel is the penetrating judgment of those who in the midst of brute and black rock pretend to see a vein of fine gold. The annals of human perspicacity contain no greater miracle of intuition. Just what chance do the geniuses who put forth a military candidate give to the Constitution squeezed as it will be between the blade and the scabbard?

A political platform is a profession of faith in action. The faith that is professed, when the lips do not lie, is what is in the heart, beliefs, and ideas. But the ideas, beliefs, and the heart of man manifest themselves in his life. His acts are the mirror of his conscience, the reflection of his sentiments, the language of his convictions. Now, cast your glance over that career of arms, easy, accelerated, tranquil; follow its phases one by one; count one by one the incidents. You will not point out to me one instance, one moment, one trace where it was anything more than the career of a soldier: obedience, discipline, command; military aptitudes, qualities, preoccupations, and interests. Those preoccupations and interests, those qualities and aptitudes are the ones that make a man of one, not the ones that create a man of law, a man of government, a statesman.

.   .   .

In all my life never did I see take shape such a grave situation in the sight of my moral eyes, so antagonistic to the articles of my old creed, as this one devoid even of the guarantee of a responsible sword and of the least military prestige such as Deodoro da Fonseca or Floriano Peixoto possessed when they surrendered to the anarchy of ambition. We see it approaching aided and abetted by the weakness, intrigue, vulgarity, and consciencelessness of the civilian government and partisan factions.

It was because of the sudden alarm of this imminent danger that the August Convention met. In it all other considerations, all other preoccupations, all other apprehensions were put aside in order to propose, as the exclusive objective of this movement, as the specific function of the candidate who represents it, a reaction against the rebirth of militarism. The nation, in its most civilized elements, has a more than justified fear of that contingency impending upon us thanks to the criminal complicity of the Nilo Peçanha administration, the oligarchies of the North, and a majority in the National Congress ready to submit to military authoritarianism. Before this great danger all other questions disappear. There is only one problem on the horizon. It exclusively dominates the entire perspective of the future. Here we see the incomparable proportions of this movement which has no parallel in the history of Brazil.

THE HEADACHE OF COFFEE (1911)

Coffee, one of Brazil's great agricultural resources, has also proved at may times to be one of its major economic problems. The Brazilian side of the problem was its prolonged effort to bring a profitable return to the immense coffee industry, expecially in the state of São Paulo. The American side (or one should say the consumer's side, wherever that consumer might be found) lay in the attempt to make the product available at a reasonable price.

Brazil's coffee valorization program was only one of several efforts made in that country to assure favorable prices to the producer. Efforts were made at certain times to burn the surplus amounts or to take them to sea and dump them. At other times Brazil tried using coffee surpluses as fuel for locomotives and also attempted, largely unsuccessfully, to convert them into plastics. But coffee still remains a Brazilian economic headache.

The following document is extracted from a report that was made by a specialist in the U.S. Department of Justice, William T. Chantland, dated September 6, 1911. It was published in Papers Relating to the Foreign Relations of the United States for 1913.

...The world now consumes a million and half bags of coffee, of 60 kilos each, per month, or 198,000,000 pounds of coffee per month, or 18,000,000 bags, with a total of over two and one-third billion pounds of coffee per year. Of this, the United States consumes 40 per cent of the entire amount, or about 80,000,000 pounds per month, or 950,000,000 pounds per year...

For the coffee year from July 1, 1910, to June 30, 1911, the world's crop of coffee for the first time fell far below the world's consumption. It was fourteen and one-half million bags, or a shortage of three and one-half million bags on the world's consumption for the year. Of the world's coffee the Republic of Brazil produces from 80 to 85 per cent, and of the Brazilian coffee the great bulk is produced in the two large States of São Paulo and Rio.

It will appear clearly, therefore, that anything which affects coffee in Brazil must immediately be felt in the United States, which consumes 40 per cent of all the world's coffee and which buys and consumes from 80 to 85 per cent of the Brazilian coffee. In 1906-7 the world's crop of coffee was unusually large, being estimated at about 22,000,000 bags. The Minister of Finance of the State of São Paulo conceived or stood sponsor for a plan as to coffee, something like the once proposed populistic plan of making wheat the standard of value. This coffee plan has become known as the "Valorization of coffee," and the State reports, published at lenght on it, are spoken of as "Transactions in the defense of coffee."

"Valorization," as defined in the consular reports of our consul, means to give, by law, a fictitious or artificial value above or apart from the normal or ordinary market value. That the sole intent of the valorization plan from its conception and inception was to artificially enhance the price of the staple, coffee, above its natural or market price, there is now no longer any room for doubt, and I do not see that there ever should have been any real question on that score. What other object can either excuse or explain the attempt, let alone justify it?

That the desired objects have been attained pari passu with the dreams of their originators is also now apparent. However, there are still some who profess to think that natural causes and not valorization are responsible for the recent rise and doubling in the price of coffee.

On the questions both of the intention and result of the valorization plan, as a plan to raise the price of coffee, let us overlook for a moment Minister Egydio's naive disclaimer of any further interest on the part of his Government in the plan, as set forth in his cable of April 1, 1909,....

Let the editor of the Brazilian Review, who was against the plan to begin with, from economic reasons, as a Brazilian, offer his testimony as to the object and result of the plan from the South American standpoint.

> The action of the São Paulo Government in promoting valorization has been condemned because it succeeded, against all expectations, in putting up prices and so, incidentally, raising the cost of coffee to consumers.
>
> Surprising as it may seem, this was indeed the very end and aim of its existence.

Here again is good testimony of what the aim and result was and is.

The law and declared policy in the United States is that value shall be the result only of natural market conditions of supply and demand and competition, and that anything which seeks to and does fix prices artificially at a different level is frowned upon and made illegal in most States by statute, and illegal by Federal statute where such artificially fixed prices are the direct result of any contract or combination or conspiracy...

To make effective this plan of coffee valorization it was necessary to have the aid of powerful financiers, and conditions demanded by them had to be met. As Minister Egydio puts it, in his cable of April 1, 1909, measure "created by exigency (demand) of the bankers," but which "the Government is negotiating with them to replace it by another more acceptable to the markets." This report is only interested with such financiers so far as they may be citizens of the United States.

At the beginning several agreements were entered into between the three Brazilian States of Rio, Minas Geraes, and São Paulo, in accordance with which edicts were published to make the agreements effective, which contained among their provisions one for the curtailment and restriction by law of further coffee planting "by a sufficiently high tax," while the three States should mutually agree. These laws are still effective, and the additional planting of coffee trees stopped in 1906. Naturally when the planting was stopped every owner of coffee trees tried to make those which he had planted and growing produce to the utmost, and they were attended to properly, with the one good result that the quality of coffee grown was probably bettered. However, when the limited production thus made possible had been reached, the increase in the production of coffee must stop. On the other hand, the world's consumption of coffee has steadily increased. Thus there would come a time --

and it has already arrived -- when coffee consumption annually exceeds coffee production. And when such a condition of affairs arrives and continues for a time, as it soon will, it is apparent that any man, or group of men, or financiers, who control any appreciable percentage of the world's visible supply of coffee are in a position to exact any price they desire for what they have on hand. In other words, if such restraint over the market and coffee trade as to be able to arbitratily control and fix the price of coffee. This exact contigency was foreseen and calculated on in the conception of the valorization plan. Whether the financiers and their coffee-trading associates took any active steps to induce the making of these restrictive laws or not, the fact remains that such laws were either in existence and known at the time or enacted subsequently by demand of the bankers, and formed a part of the scheme of security by future enhancement of price under which the loans were made and accepted and made secure to the financiers...

Under the valorization plan purchase of coffee for the account of the government of São Paulo was begun August 20, 1906, through several banking and coffee firms, among them Crossman & Sielcken, of New York City, a partnership composed of George W. Crossman and Herman Sielcken...

By a special contract executed in London, December 11, 1908, the entire conduct of the valorization scheme for the benefit of the State and the financiers, was intrusted to a committee of seven members, of which Herman Sielcken, of the firm of Crossman & Sielcken, New York City, who had originally represented the National City Band as its authorized agent in the negotiations for the three million pounds loan of 1906, was and is yet the American member...

In the agreement relative to the committee dated London, December 11, 1908, made between representatives of all the bankers having to do with the loan and the Government of Sao Paulo, article 2 is as follows:

A. The Government of São Paulo now obligates itself to offer for sale, through the committee, at public auctions or by sealed proposals, at the price of the day, preferably during the last six months of the coffee crop, i. e., from January to June 30: 500,000 bags in 1909-10, 600,000 bags in 1910-11, 700,000 bags in 1912-13, etc., and 700,000 bags each following year.

B. In consequence the Government expressly concedes to the committee full and irrevocable power to determine the times of sale, the minimum obligatory quantities above mentioned, the markets in which to sell, and to make the sales in the name of the Government, exercise control over the transactions, and generally to do what is required...

In plain English, this whole thing looks like a plan devised in the apparent interest of São Paulo and Brazil, but, in fact, carried out to the great glory and financial profit of Baron Schroeder, the National City Bank, and their subsequently allied banks, and accomplished through the probably honest, patriotic motives and sense of São Paulo's financial minister, Egydio Aranha, who, in his official reports, sets out enthusiastically how it all happened, and how they were able to pay loan after loan by making new loans, each one larger and each negotiated at a greater disadvantage, discount, and loss to the State, and, consequently, a resulting new and bigger profit to the eminent international financiers and their coffee-trade friends...

If there might be those who would conjure up any halos for those members of the committee, let me cite them to the action of the committee as officially reported by themselves of their meeting of April 27, 1909, wherein "the committee, after careful consideration of all interests, is of opinion that the proposed change of the law is desirable." which proposed the "replacement of the existing law limiting the export of coffee by a new law creating an extra duty of 10 per cent on all exports of coffee, payable in kind, such coffee to be destroyed under the control of the committee," and which went so far as to consider whether said coffee should be burned or carried out on shipboard and dropped into the sea.

Speculation as to whether, without valorization, the jobbing price of coffee would now be higher, as some opine, is purposeless to this inquiry, because without valorization and attendant restrictions upon the areas of cultivation, the conditions as to supply can not now be known, but the normal guess would be that the supply would now be ample: that is, that the increase in acreage of cultivation would have kept pace with the increase in consumption in coffee as it does in most matters, instead of having ceased at reaching the limit under trees recently planted and their better cultivation, as reported. And it is not sound argument on that side to say that valorization saved the planters from ruin and the plantations from going into the hands of the bankers. It is but common experience that what goes into the hands of bankers is only under their greater keenness to have their property and plantations well and fully cared for and cultivated.

Likewise, other planters would naturally have been diverted to the development of new plantations. We, however, have only to deal with the situation as it is, with the crop area restricted, the utmost increasing. Already have we this year reached a situation where the world's production is considerably less than its consumption... In other words, approximately half of the world's small visible supply is now in the control of the valorization committee, composed of the strongest and most powerful coffee men and their allies and the financiers back of them. The mere suggestion of this fact must make it apparent how thoroughly at the mercy of this valorization committee is the price of our coffee. Add to this condition the fact that valorization has still more than seven years to run, with continual increase of consumption and no prospect for any large increase in production -- at least within seven years, as it takes six full years for new trees, if any were planted immediately, to bear any substantial amount of coffee -- and the danger and iniquity of the situation and the power of the valorization committee appalls...

The members of the committee, and the financiers for whom they are agents, are certainly day by day and year by year restraining trade in coffee by holding out these 6,000,000 bags. Moreover, the very essence of this plan, in which they engaged and are engaging was to valorize or cause an artificial, or fixed, or made price on coffee, higher than the natural or ordinary open-market price.

Again, the committee and those in control of the coffee are not even true to their trust so far as the State of São Paulo is concerned, because their minister of finance cabled the Brazilian ambassador here, at the time of the attempt to place a proposed import duty on coffee by Congress in 1909, to the effect that all of the coffee could be sold when it had reached the price of 47 francs per bag of 50 kilos, or the equivalent 56.4 francs per bag of 60 kilos. Instead of that, they are now holding the coffee at a price far above that, the last sales, in April, having been made at about 73 to 75 francs per bag of 60 kilos.

The only good points, from the standpoint of the American public, in the plan are possibly the two following:

(1) It has steadied the market and prevented useless, reckless speculation. Whether the steadying and fixing of the market is a good thing is a question. The theory is, in this country, that the market should be open and unsteady, and inviting to free and open competition; so this may be a questionable benefit after all.

(2) It has probably improved the average quality of coffee, in that the restriction of planting made them cultivate more carefully.

The new results of the valorization appear to be:

(1) Large profits to the financiers.

(2) Some net profit to the planters.

(3) None to the State; rather a loss because of the amount of revenue, the collection of which is called for and diverted, and, while the State's coffee is going up in price, yet it is probable that the interest, storage, and commission charges will eat that up before the end of the valorization scheme, January 1, 1919.

(4) The addition and piling of all these costs and advances on the coffee consumers.

(5) The restraint in trade caused by the carrying out of the plan.

(6) The enhancement of the price of the great article of common use imported chiefly from Brazil -- coffee...

In this case I would recommend that, as a part of the proceedings, instructions be given to institute seizure and condemnation proceedings on the first valorization coffee to move in interstate commerce. I do not believe it would require but one such seizure to enable the Government to make terms as to the future handling and disposition of valorization coffee...

Moreover, the Government of São Paulo, through the Brazilian Government, has officially disclaimed further interest in the valorization operations. In an official message to the secretary of the Brazilian embassy at Washington, sent for the purpose of influencing the official actions of the Congress of the United States, and sent through the Brazilian Government's official channels, the minister of finance of São Paulo, under date of April 1, 1909, said:

The Government of São Paulo is no longer engaged in any valorization operations and has ceased entirely with its intervention in the market with the signing of the 15,000,000 pounds sterling loan. All the coffee stock belonging to the State has been delivered to the committee of bankers authorized to sell it. The committee is obliged to sell, in accordance with the contract, at the market price and to the amount of 500,000 bags during the year 1909-10,

600,000 bags during the year 1910-11, and 700,000 bags during the year 1912-13, and an equal amount in the following years. The committee can, however, sell all or any coffee as soon as the price will reach 47 francs per 50 kilos of good average.

There is therefore no action of this Government to advance the price of coffee, as its whole stock can be sold within a few years at the market price. On the contrary, it limits the rise of the market to the maximum price of 47 francs (equivalent to 56.4 francs per ordinary bag of 60 kilos), by which all stock can be sold at once, that price being hardly sufficient to cover the cost of production in the finest coffee zones of this State.

And then, in order that there might be no question at all as to the Stat's disinterestedness, he proceeds with his disclaimer by putting the burden of causing the export duty to be levied by his State on coffee upon the bankers who financed the cheme...

A failure on the part of this Department to prosecute this matter to the utmost would rightfully bring down upon it the censure of the people, for whom it constitutes the machinery which must stand between them and such unconscionable, open, high-handed, continuous, and bold violation of law for the express and only purpose, from the very conception and inception of the scheme, of gouging the consuming public of this country to the extent of all the numerous commissions and charges which the scheme involved, to the profit of the high financiers of international operation, plus whatever profit which was to come to this foreign nation and its people, at the expense of the American consuming public, who are the known customers of from 80 to 85 per cent of their entire product... The law is plain. The intent is plain -- there has been but one purpose from the beginning. The results are apparent. The future results, unless checked, will be appalling.

If any steps taken bring on negotiations with the Brazilian States, the persons who are conducting them should under no circumstances forget to have the removal of planting restrictions in mind, as a part of the remedy desired, so that the increase of area may again at least begin to grow with the continuing increase in consumption. Even then the situation on that point will be very bad before the remedy can become effective because of the six-year term required for coffee trees to come into fruition. The urgency of the promptest kind of action is apparent.

VARGAS AND THE NEW STATE (1937)

A good case can probably be made that Getúlio Vargas was one of the most influential two men in the history of independent Brazil, the other of course being the Emperor Dom Pedro II. The high point of Vargas' career doubtless came on November 10, 1937, the date on which he abolished the constitution of 1934, suspended congress and all state legislatures, and instituted a peculiarly personal rule under the guise of the Estado Novo (New State). The documentary monument of this second phase of Vargas' rule was the new constitution which he promulgated on the date of his coup, November 10. The reputed author of the new basic law was Francisco Campos, Vargas' minister of justice, but in all likelihood Vargas himself was its chief author.

The 1937 constitution was one of the most unusual that any of the Latin American nations have written among the more than 200 that have been drafted since their independence. It was the product of much political stress and strain in the years from 1935 to 1937. In the preamble Vargas conveniently placed the blame on the Communists, who deserved some, but not all, of it. Ostensibly the new law maintained Brazil as a federation but, in an effort to strengthen the underpinnings of his own power, Vargas concentrated vast authority in national hands and, at all levels, in the persons of executive officials rather than legislative bodies or courts. Indeed, some students of government doubted that Brazil remained a federation except in a nominal sense. Instances of the shift of power toward national and executive authorities were numerous, ingenious, and extreme. Extracts illustrative of such a shift are given below, taken from an English translation of the constitution published in 1937 by the Brazilian government press department.

Preamble

The President of the Republic of the United States of Brazil:

Whereas, the legitimate aspiration of the Brazilian people for political and social peace, seriously disturbed by manifest factors of disorder, created by growing party dissensions, which a malicious demagogic propaganda attempted to transform into class warfare, and which, through the extreme force attained by the ideological conflicts, tended, in its natural process of development, to solve itself by violence, thus subjecting the Nation to the imminent threat of civil war;

Whereas, the state of apprehension caused throughout the Country by the infiltration of communism, which was growing daily more widespread and deeper, calls for a remedy both radical and permanent in character;

Whereas, the previously existing institutions did not supply the State with normal means for preserving and defending its peace, the safety and well being of the people;

With the support of the armed forces and yielding to the dictates of public opinion, both justifiably apprehensive of the dangers threatening our unity and of the swiftness with which our civil and political institutions were being undermined;

Resolves to insure to the Nation its unity, the respect of its honor and of its independence, and to the Brazilian people, under a regime of political and social peace, the necessary conditions for their security, their welfare and their prosperity;

Decreeing the following Constitution, which comes into effect as from this date, throughout the Country:

CONSTITUTION OF THE UNITED STATES OF BRAZIL

The National Organization

Article 1. Brazil is a Republic. Political power emanates from the people and is exercised in their name and in the interest of their well-being, their honor, their independence, and their prosperity.

Art. 2. The use of the national flag, hymn, coat-of-arms and shield is obligatory throughout the country. There will be no other flags, hymns, shields and coats-of-arms. The use of these national symbols will be regulated by law. . . .

Art. 8. Each State is to organize its own services to meet its own particular interests and must pay for them out of its own resources.

Sole paragraph. A State which for three consecutive years fails to collect sufficient revenue to maintain these services will be transformed into a Territory, until its financial capacity is reestablished.

Art. 9. The Federal Government may intervene in the States, through the nomination, by the President of the Republic, of an interventor, who will assume in the State those functions which, according to its Constitution, belong to the Executive Power, or those which, in accordance with the necessities and the requirements of each case, are given him by the President of the Republic. . . .

Art. 11. A law, when initiated by Parliament, will be limited to regulate the matter in general terms, passing only upon the substance and principles which constitute its object. The Executive Power will issue the complementary regulations.

Art. 12. The President of the Republic may be authorized by the Parliament to issue decree-laws in accordance with the conditions and within the limits fixed by the act of authorization.

Art. 13. The President of the Republic, during the recess of Parliament or during the dissolution of the Chamber of Deputies, may, if the necessities of the State require such action, issue decree-laws regarding material within the legislative capacity of the Union, excepting [eight exceptions]. . . .

Art. 14. The President of the Republic, when complying with the dispositions of the Constitution and within the limits of the respective budget appropriations, may freely issue decree-laws regarding the organization of the Government and of the Federal Administration, the supreme command and the organization of the armed forces. . . .

Art. 19. The law may establish what services, under the jurisdiction of the Federal Government, may be executed by the States; in this case the Federal Executive Power will issue the regulations and instructions which the States must observe in carrying out these services. . . .

Art. 22. The States may enter into agreements with the Federal Government to delegate to Union officials the execution of laws, services, acts or decisions of their governments. . . .

Art. 24. The States may create other forms of taxation. Double taxation is, however, forbidden, and the tax decreed by the Union will prevail where the jurisdiction is concurrent. It is within the province of the Federal Council, either on its own initiative or at the request of the tax payer, to declare that there is double taxation, and suspend the collection of the State tax. . . .

The Legislative Power

Art. 38. The Legislative Power is exercised by the National Parliament, with the cooperation of the National Economic Council and that of the President of the Republic; the former by means of opinions and recommendations concerning subjects within its consultative competency, and the latter by the initiative and sanction of the projects and the promulgation of the decree-laws authorized by this Constitution.

Sec. 1. The National Parliament is composed of two Chambers: the Chamber of Deputies and the Federal Council. . . . [The elaborate provisions following, dealing with legislative machinery and operation, became pointless because the congress was never activated during the Estado Novo; all legislation was by executive decree.]

Art. 46. The Chamber of Deputies is composed of representatives of the people, elected by indirect suffrage. . . .

Art. 50. The Federal Council is composed of representatives of the States and ten members nominated by the President of the Republic. . . .

Art. 59. The National Economic Council will be presided over by a Minister of State, designated by the President of the Republic.

Sec. 1. The President of the Republic will also have the power to appoint three members of each section of the National Economic Council. . . .

Art. 63. At any time, power may be vested in the National Economic Council, through a plebiscite to be regulated by law, to legislate on certain or all matters pertaining to their special province.

Sole paragraph. The initiative in calling the plebiscite will be within the power of the President of the Republic, who will specify in the respective decree the conditions under which and the matters upon which the National Economic Council may legislate.

Laws and Resolutions

Art. 64. The initiative for all projects [i.e., bills] belongs in principle to the Government. In no case, can any project of amendment be discussed if it concerns taxation or if it would result in an increase in expenditures.

Sec. 1. No one member may initiate a project of law. This initiative may only be taken by one-third of the Deputies or of the members of the Federal Council.

Sec. 2. Any project initiated in either of the Chambers will be suspended as soon as the Government communicates its intention of presenting a project treating the same matter. . . .

The President of the Republic

Art. 73. The President of the Republic, the supreme authority of the State, will coordinate the activities of the representative organs, direct internal and external policy, and promote or direct the legislative policy deemed best for the Nation's interests, and supervise the administration of the Country. . . .

Art. 75. The following are prerogatives of the President of the Republic:

(a) To nominate one of the candidates to the Presidency of the Republic; . . . .

Art. 84. The Electoral Collage shall meet in the Capital of the Republic twenty days before the expiration of the presidential term of office and shall choose its candidate for the Presidency of the Republic. In the event the President does not use his prerogative of indicating a candidate, the choice of the Electoral College shall be declared elected.

Sole paragraph. In the event of the President of the Republic indicating a candidate, the election shall be by direct and universal suffrage, between the two candidates. . . .

[A number of social and economic provisions either foreshadowed the elaboration of such concepts in the Argentine constitution of 1949 or reflected the impact of provisions in the Mexican constitution of 1917]:

Art. 124. The family, constituted by indissoluble marriage, is under special protection of the State. Large families will be granted compensation in proportion to their necessities. . . .

Art. 132. The State will found institutions or will give assistance and protection to those founded by civic associations, with the object of organizing for the youth annual periods of work in the fields and workshops, so as to promote moral discipline and physical development, in such a manner as to fit them to fulfill their duties toward the well-being and defense of the Nation. . . .

Art. 136. Labor is a social duty. Intellectual, technical and manual labor has a right to the protection and special care of the State. . . .

Art. 143. Mines and other sub-soil wealth, as well as waterfalls, constitute property distinct from ownership of the soil for purposes of production or industrial use. The industrial use of mines and mineral deposits, of streams and water-power, even when privately owned, is dependent on Federal authorization. . . .

Art. 144 The law will regulate the progressive nationalization of mines, mineral deposits, and waterfalls or other sources of power, as well as those industries considered basic or essential to the economic or military defense of the Nation. . . .

The Defense of the State

Art. 166. . . .
Once it becomes necessary to use the armed forces for the defense of the State, The President of the Republic shall declare a state of war for the whole National Territory or part thereof. . . .
Art. 171. During the existence of a state of war the Constitution ceases to be in force in those parts indicated by the President of the Republic. . . .

Amendments to the Constitution

Art. 174. This Constitution may be amended, modified or altered through the initiative of either the President of the Republic or of the Chamber of Deputies.
Sec. 1. When the project is brought before Parliament on the initiative of the President of the Republic, it must be voted en bloc by an ordinary majority vote of the Chamber of Deputies and of the Federal Council, without any changes or with such modifications as have been proposed by the President of the Republic, or which have his approval, if suggested by either of the Chambers. . . .

THE STRAINS OF A WAR -- IN PROSPECT AND AT HAND (1932-1945)

The decades of the 1930s and 1940s were especially critical for Brazil -- and for that country's relations with the United States -- because, among other things, of the approach, and then the presence, of World War II. It was a conflict whose forewarning clouds could be seen years before 1939 when the storm actually broke, and 1941 when it reached the Western Hemisphere.

The key to much of what happened in those eventful years was Nazi Germany, whose führer, Adolf Hitler, came to power in January, 1933, and which then began an aggressive commercial, political, diplomatic, and military policy which culminated in the holocaust of 1939-45. Brazil, too, had a dynamic leader; Getulio Vargas had come to power in October, 1930, and, while capable of equivocation, moved generally to unify and advance Brazilian interests. In the United States this period of flux brought its own dynamism into office in the person of Franklin Roosevelt, who was inaugurated only a few weeks after Hitler assumed power. Thus three strong men in three important countries were shaping destinies which reached far beyond their own lands.

Before the interplay of world politics could get under full way however, Brazil had internal problems to resolve. One of the chief of these was the smoldering resentment in São Paulo which in 1932 flared into revolt. It became a civil war which required some three months to suppress.

It was the unfolding drama of international politics, however, which primarily occupied hemispheric and, indeed, world attention. Germany's first avenue toward achieving her place in the sun was an aggressive trade policy designed to further German foreign commerce, especially at the expense of British and American world trade. One of the gambits used in this campaign was the device of the "blocked mark," a controlled currency intended to channel more foreign trade toward Germany. The negotiations over exchange arrangements became highly complex and involved and occupied United States government officials at many stages.

A more dramatic aspect of the growing international rivalry was the effort to contain and then reduce German aviation activity in Latin America. Such activity had been expanding since soon after World War I and under the Nazis grew explosively. The coming of World War II to the hemisphere in December, 1941, led in a few weeks to the convening of the Third Foreign Ministers' Conference at Rio de Janeiro in January, 1942, where the United States delegation was headed by Undersecretary of State Sumner Welles. Momentous problems had to be solved. The basic upshot was the decision, acceded to by all states except Argentina and Chile, for a severance of Axis diplomatic relations by all hemispheric countries not yet involved in the war. Following the war came the question of what should be done about maintaining Brazil's defense posture at a high level.

All these matters (and of course many others) were treated in the diplomatic correspondence of the United States and Brazil. The following documents, from Papers Relating to the Foreign Relations of the United States of the years as the dates indicate, elaborate on the details of some of the major problems.

The Chargé in Brazil (Thurston) to the Secretary of State

Rio de Janeiro, July 15,1932.

[Received July 25.]

Sir: In amplification of the Embassy's telegraphic reports during the last few days, I have the honor to inform the Department as follows with respect to the insurrection now in progress in the State of São Paulo:

Review

While various factors have contributed to the present situation, its immediate causes may be said to have been the ineptitude displayed by the Provisional Government in its treatment of the proud and powerful State of São Paulo, the conflict between the politicians and the military or "Tenente" element of the Administration, and the delay in the return to constitutional government.

For almost two years, as Consul General Cameron's able reports will have made evident to the Department, the State of São Paulo, defeated in the 1930 revolution, has been maintained in a condition of irritating political uncertainty and subjected to arbitrary military control, with the result that the habitually strong sectional feeling of the Paulistas has been provoked to the point of apparently unanimous rebellion. It is not to be doubted, of course, that the political organization overthrown by the 1930 revolution has sought to benefit by these conditions -- but that the abuses were great is indicated by the fact that the State political party originally supporting the Administration joined forces with those of the old regime in the formation of a United Front (Frente Unica) for the defense of the rights of the State.

The Tenente problem resulted from the necessity which confronted the victorious revolutionists in 1930 of replacing the entire personnel of the deposed Government with supporters of the new régime. Many of the appointees -- even State Interventors -- were necessarily young officers (Lieutenants, or Tenentes) whose inexperience was outweighed by their loyalty. Rivalry between these officers (the Tenente group, of course, likewise embraces many civilians) and the political leaders inevitably developed, as a result of inherently divergent policies, until it assumed a character of the utmost gravity. It must be recalled, in this connection, that the revolution of 1930 was not exclusively an uprising of one political party against the one in power, but was a movement of States, largely transcending local party sentiment and designed to break the control of one powerful State -- São Paulo -- then in power and supported momentarily by the arms of the Nation. Thus it was, for example, that at the beginning the present Government had the full collaboration of the State of Rio Grande do Sul, the local contending parties having united in the revolution and each having contributed members to the administration.

As the divergent policies of the two groups became defined, it was apparent that the political element advocated the early termination of the provisional government and the return to normal constitutional government through elections, whereas the Tenente element considered that the fruits of victory would be lost unless the elections should be postponed until the political organization of the old régime had been certainly destroyed. It was in consequence a logical development for the Tenentes to come to regard the "pro-constitutionalization" program of the political parties as merely a cloak for the efforts of the old regime to regain control.

Throughout his administration, President Vargas has adopted a policy of opportunism designed to conciliate as much as possible the conflicting tendencies within his government. It was not probable, however, that he could indefinitely pursue such a course with success, and although he permitted the destruction of a Rio de Janeiro newspaper by the Tenentes to go unpunished (thereby so offending the political parties that the support of his own State was withdrawn), but acquiesced in an adjustment of the São Paulo problem in a manner constituting a defeat for the Tenentes, only later to refuse the demands of the political parties that the Government be reorganized in a manner to lessen the power of the Tenentes, the practice of balancing favors and rebuffs weakened confidence in his leadership. The failure of this policy followed the President's effort to appease both the "immediate constitutionalization" and "postponement" organizations when, in apparent deference to the former, he promulgated last May (a year and a half after taking over the Government) a Decree providing for the holding of a Constituent Assembly, but offset that concession by fixing the date for the Constituent Assembly one year in the future, in May, 1933. Both sides may have been expected by him to be gratified by this arrangement, but the politicians saw in the further delay only a victory for the Tenentes, and they had no confidence in a plan which failed to set a date, after the holding of the Constituent Assembly, for the actual election of new supreme authorities.

To summarize the foregoing, then, it may be said that the Vargas Government came into power with general approbation, and that had elections been called within a reasonable period after the victorious revolution it is probable that the revolutionary candidates and their principles would have prevailed. The long delay in the return to constitutional government, and the errors that were committed caused the early enthusiasm to wane and animosities to be created, with the result that the old politicians, momentarily dispersed and discredited, have been able to reestablish themselves. If the São Paulo revolution is victorious, it is to be presumed that the new Government will be largely formed and controlled by the old political regime.

The Revolution

With respect to the immediate situation, it is not possible, in the absence of trustworthy information, to formulate a sound opinion. The Minister for Foreign Affairs informed me, and his statements have been repeated by others, that the revolution was premature, it having been prepared to take place on July 14 as a simultaneous uprising in São Paulo, Minas Geraes, Rio Grande do Sul, and the City of Rio de Janeiro. The indiscretion of a young conspirator in São Paulo in communicating a seditious message to Rio Grande do Sul by radio, and the suspicious activities of the military commander in Matto Grosso (General Klinger -- now with São Paulo) warned the Government of the danger and forced the revolutionists in São Paulo to strike before they had intended. The Government, by immediately taking the requisite measures in the threatened districts, was enabled to prevent the general outbreak which had been contemplated. Assuming this information to be accurate, as I do, it is obvious that the revolutionists had support in the places named, which, despite repressive measures, may be assumed still to exist and to constitute a potential danger to the Vargas Government.

The tactics of the Government, as has been reported, are designed to isolate São Paulo, preventing it from receiving cooperation from other sections of the Republic, and so to circumscribe it as to bring about the collapse of the movement without bloodshed, if possible. To this end, instead of engaging in immediate attack upon the State, troops are being concentrated on the frontiers in large numbers, presumably with the intention of accumulating such a preponderant military force as to make any eventual aggressive measures reasonably certain of success. Reinforcements have arrived from some of the northern States, and others are expected from Rio Grande do Sul. It is officially stated, and apparently correctly, that Minas Geraes and Paraná are collaborating with the Government. Minor skirmishes have occurred, but no general offensive seems yet to be underway.

Possible Developments

In speculating upon the possibilities of the present situation, the following contingencies may be considered:

a) The balance of power rests with the States of Minas Geraes and Rio Grande do Sul. If they voluntarily or by constraint remain with the Government São Paulo may be forced to capitulate;

b) A coup d'état in Rio de Janeiro might occur;

c) A similar occurrence might take place in Minas Geraes or Rio Grande do Sul, throwing their support to São Paulo;

d) The São Paulo forces, being well armed and apparently inspired by a cause, might inflict a decisive defeat upon the Government forces.

Respectfully yours,   Walter C. Thurston

The Ambassador in Brazil (Gibson) to the Secretary of State

Rio de Janeiro, June 6, 1936 -- 7 p.m.

[Received June 7 -- 7 a.m.]

In the course of a conversation this morning Macedo Soares handed me the following memorandum intended as a reply to the aide-mémoire handed by the Department to Aranha on June 1st.

"Memorandum. 1. The Brazilian Government received with pleasure and examined with the most detailed and friendly attention the memorandum which the Embassy of the United States presented to it in the name of its Government on Thursday of information furnished by the Minister Macedo Soares to Ambassador Gibson regarding the commercial negotiations under way between Brazil and Germany.

2. In this document the American Government drawing attention at the start to the fact that 'the precise text of the proposed agreement between Germany and Brazil has not yet been received' -- which moreover it could not have been as the matter had not yet reached the point of a definite formula -- gives immediate[ly] to understand that its comments are not intended to express any opinion as to the practical effects that such an agreement might cause to the prejudice or benefit of American commerce in Brazil which obviously places the comment offered upon a theoretical basis of principle.

3. It is extremely agreeable to the Brazilian Government in these conditions to hasten to affirm to the Embassy of the United States for information of the American Government the fullest explanations best calculated to dissipate any apprehension which may have arisen or which it would involve from any ill-founded interpretation as to the consequences of the negotiations now under way between Brazil and Germany might have for the maintenance and development of the policy of free commerce endorsed in the Brazilian-American treaty of February 2, 1935.

4. Under these conditions the Brazilian Government desires, before that the return to the broadest liberal principles for equality of opportunities and of treatment for the commerce of all nations combined with the reduction or gradual elimination of the many restrictions which now asphyxiate it, is the only sure way if not the only way to bring about return to the prosperity of international commerce; and finally seeing in these principles more than the mere everything else to reaffirm here once again its unalterable conviction that as the American Government so well says in the memorandum under acknowledgement it is in the system of compensation and of narrow bilateralism that we find one of the principle obstacles to the restoration and expansion of international commerce so urgently needed by the world. Furthermore the Brazilian Government shares without reservation the conviction [of?] the importance of a simple commercial policy. The Brazilian Government continues to believe as does the Government of the United States that from the application of these principles based on a broader view there is bound to result not only for the prosperity of the world but also and above all for universal peace, the most brilliant hope.

5. Consequently it is without hesitation that the Brazilian Government once more affirms its fidelity to these ideas not only in the limited field of commercial activity but also and chiefly in the broader domain of general international policy.

6. Once these basic and essential points have been thus clarified the Brazilian Government feels disposed to declare that in its negotiations with Germany its purposes have not gone beyond what is clearly defined in the following terms by the American memorandum: 'In the existing exigencies of trade and international payments there may be room for barter transactions for the exchange of specific commodities on fair terms offering mutual advantage. Such transactions negotiated between non-governmental producer or distributors of merchandise even though facilitated by governments though obviously an inefficient procedure suitable only when normal monetary facilities are unavailing may not be objectionable in principle.'

7. It was precisely upon conception of this character that the Brazilian Government based its present negotiations with Germany allowing herself to proceed with these because of the imperative requirements and the real necessities of its international commerce and seeking to confine them within a provisional formula which without violating the general policy which it has adopted and from which it does not propose to deviate, would permit it to meet the needs of certain immediate interests.

8. The determining factor in these negotiations was the necessity for the sale to Germany of a part of the Brazilian cotton crop. The Germans definitely require this product. If we were not to meet their request we ran a serious risk of not disposing of certain of our other articles (among them coffee) in that important market. In order to insure the German market for these products the Brazilian Government agreed on the basis of payment in the same exchange in which other articles had been paid for, that is in compensation marks, to deliver a quantity of cotton equivalent to 62,000 tons annually. In exchange for this concession the German Government was prepared to give certain specified facilities to our export trade in general. The intervention of the Brazilian Government consists therefore barely in agreeing to recognize the purchasing power of compensation marks for the financing of a provisional agreement of this character applying chiefly to cotton, an arrangement the execution of which will be entirely in the hands of the interested parties.

9. Under such conditions the Brazilian Government can unhesitatingly assure the American Government that in conformity with its wishes and hopes the American Government may rest fully assured that the provisions of any commercial agreement into which the Government of Brazil may enter with Germany will prove to be in complete accord with the principle of the policy above mentioned and will not permit the impression to be created that the Government of Brazil is in any sense compromising the position which it has so helpfully and resolutely maintained.''

Gibson

The Ambassador in Brazil (Gibson) to the Secretary of State

Rio de Janeiro, June 6, 1936 -- 8 p.m.

[Received June 7 -- 1:54 a.m.]

After handing me the memorandum transmitted in my 146, June 6, 7 p.m., Macedo Soares told me that on more careful examination it had proved to be impossible to find any method for reconciling in the form of even a temporary agreement the needs of the German system of directed economy and the Brazilian system of free commerce and that consequently the idea of the provisional German-Brazilian trade agreement had been abandoned.

He stated that two steps would be taken in the near future:

1. The Brazilian Ambassador in Germany will address a note to the German Government stating that the Brazilian Government will permit purchases for compensation marks of Brazilian cotton to a maximum amount of 62,000 tons staggered over a 12 months period. The Brazilian action is unilateral and equivalent to the placing of a Brazilian export quota on cotton in exchange for compensation marks and makes it clear that any purchases above this amount must be paid for in currency of international acceptance. Once this is done Macedo anticipates that the German Government will announce import quotas on various Brazilian products.

Inasmuch as the Germans bought 82,000 tons of cotton last year Macedo believes that to meet their needs they will be obliged to buy at least that amount this year and to pay for the surplus in international currency.

2. As the Brazilian-German trade treaty has been denounced and expires on June 30th it is necessary to take steps to maintain most-favored-nation treatment for both countries; consequently there will be an exchange of notes stating that each country recognizes to the other the right of most-favored-nation treatment pending the conclusion of a definite commercial treaty. Macedo states that he can foresee no possibility of concluding a final treaty so long as Germany continues under the compensation system and that once most-favored-nation treatment is assured it will be necessary to carry on by dint of expedients, temporary arrangements, et cetera.

Macedo states that in apprising the German Chargé d'Affaires of the difficulties in concluding a trade agreement he made a verbal communication to him to the effect that Germany must keep within normal bounds her exports to Brazil of certain products normally acquired by Brazil from countries dealing in exchange of international acceptance --which he said was equivalent to saying the United States. He informed the Chargé d'Affaires that if Germany disregarded this warning and persisted seeking unduly to enlarge her sales of motor cars, machinery, et cetera, the Brazilian Government would be obliged to "take steps." He added to me that the Brazilian Government proposed to make effective its objections to having the market flooded with German products to the detriment of normal commerce with the United States.

Gibson

The Acting Secretary of State to the Ambassador in Brazil (Caffery)
[Washington, July 30, 1940.]

Sir: In recent months the Department has been giving close attention to the commerical aviation situation in the other American republics, having in mind, first, the necessity of protecting in every possible way the maintenance and development of United States international
services; second, the probability that the majority of the other American republics will desire ultimately to have their respective domestic
and feeder line services undertaken by genuine national companies;
and third, the possibility of cooperating with such governments in the establishment of national companies through credit arrangements for the
purchase of aircraft and equipment and perhaps also for initial operations. In the last connection consideration has also been given to the
possible participation, as minority stockholders in such domestic companies, of United States carriers -- either the operators of present
international services or other United States aviation interests. The
program under discussion obviously has military, political and economic
factors of great importance both to the United States and to the other
American republics.

Consideration has already been given to urgent situations involving national defense aspects both in Colombia and in Ecuador. There
is enclosed for your confidential information a memorandum outlining
the steps taken in Colombia preliminary to the establishment of Avianca
(Aerovias Nacionales de Colombia), as a new Colombian national company to replace both Scadta (Sociedad Colombo-Alemana de Transportes
Aéreos), and Saco (Servicio Aéreo Colombiano), and on the development of the negotiations which are now in progress with the Government
of Ecuador with a view to the elimination of Sedta (Sociedad Ecuatoriana
de Transportes Aéreos).

In the light of what has been accomplished in Colombia and of
progress already made in Ecuador, the Department believes that the Brazilian aviation situation, which is obviously the most important on the
continent of South America, should now be explored. The Lufthansa
ownership of Condor and the large turnover of German pilots on Brazilian domestic airlines, the apparent delay in the enforcement of the
native pilots provisions of Brazilian legislation, the interests of Brazil
in hemisphere defense, and so on, make it desirable that consideration
be given the problem as soon as possible. At this end the Department
is already beginning discussion with Pan American Airways of the discharge of Germans from its Brazilian operations, which we regard as
urgently desirable in any case and as a condition precedent to under-
taking the general program.

Your views are therefore sought on the following points:

1. The propriety of the Embassy's approaching the Brazilian authorities on the matter at this time.

2. The probable reaction of the Brazilian Government toward a
proposal from the United States or Pan American Airways, or a combination of both, aiming to facilitate solution of

a. the financial problems involved in eliminating European (German in particular) influence (ownership, management, personnel,
et cetera) in internal Brazilian air services,

b. the technical administrative problems which would arise from discharge of European pilots and technicians, and the conversion to American equipment, and

3. The most feasible working plan for an air network offering service and facilities as good as, if not better than, what the German-controlled lines make available.
conversations you may have thereon with Brazilian Foreign Office or other officials, you may properly give due weight to the obviously great advantage to Brazil accruing from national ownership and ultimate complete national management of the country's airways now owned by Europeans, as well as the outstanding leadership and prestige which Brazil will thereby gain in the field of aviation.

Under specific directives of the White House, the Federal Loan Agency would be authorized to make to an American carrier the credits needed for the formation of Brazilian or Brazilian-American companies (with or without the participation of the Brazilian Government, at its option) to take over the German companies. The credits would be available for the initial cost of the acquisition and transfer, and would be reimbursable from Post Office Department funds paid to the American carrier receiving the technical administrative operating responsibility for the de-Germanized services from the Brazilian Government or from the newly formed company or companies. By the same decision of the President, the Civil Aeronautics Board and the Post Office Department are instructed to revise upwards mail subsidies payable to the American carrier in accordance with the new circumstances, sufficiently to cover, if necessary, operating losses on routes obviously not commercially promising for the years in the immediate future. (For your strictly confidential information: There is also under study the possibility of using in some cases nonreimbursable funds toward the attainment of some of the objectives envisioned in the aviation program.)

It is suggested that your preliminary telegraphic report on the specific points mentioned be followed by a more detailed airmail report.

Very truly yours,   Sumner Welles

The Under Secretary of State (Welles), Temporarily at Rio de Janeiro, to the Secretary of State

Rio de Janeiro, January 18, 1942 -- 6 p.m.
[Received January 19 -- 6:17 a.m.]

For the President. The highlights of the situation are approximately as follows: Two days before my arrival in Rio de Janeiro President Vargas called together his Cabinet and his highest military and naval authorities and told them that he had reached the decision that, both from the standpoint of the highest interests of Brazil as well as from the standpoint of the commitments which Brazil had previously made, Brazil must stand or fall with the United States. He stated that any member of the Government who was in disagreement with this policy was at liberty to resign his position. He received a unanimous vote of approval though the Chief of the General Staff and the Minister of War both of

whom had during the earlier months of the war been unquestionably
under the belief that Germany would triumph stated that Brazil's ability to defend herself was very limited and one of the chief reasons
for this was the fact that notwithstanding the repeated efforts which
the Brazilian Army had made to obtain armaments and munitions from
the United States and notwithstanding the repeated assurances which
had been given by the United States Government that such help would be
forthcoming, up to the present time nothing but token shipments from
the United States had been made. They stressed particularly the point
that even the few small tanks which had been sent [were without armament and were consequently practically useless. Both the Minister
for War and General Goés Monteiro, however, stated that in their considered opinion the policy announced by President Vargas was the only
correct policy for Brazil to follow. (I know from outside sources that
both Generals have made statements to exactly the same effect to representatives of the Axis Powers and to representatives of the Argentine
Chilean Governments.)

In the course of his statement of policy to his Cabinet, President
Vargas emphasized significantly that his Government did not have to
depend upon the Armed Forces of the Republic for the control of sub-
versive activities, even including any attempt at a local uprising by
German or Italian sympathizers. He told his Cabinet that the Brazilian
people were 100 per cent in agreement with the policy upon which he had
decided and that the people themselves would be able to take care of
any attempts at Axis-inspired uprisings.

Since that moment the attitude of the Brazilian Government could
not have been finer nor more firm from our point of view. The Brazilian press has cooperated completely in everything we have wanted
and the atmosphere consequently created both by the press and by open
public sympathy with the United States has needless to say been enor-
mously helpful at this time.

President Vargas has stated to the Argentine Foreign Minister
that the Brazilian Government supports the United States completely
and that the Brazilian Government considers it indispensable that a
joint declaration by all the American Republics for an immediate severance of relations with the Axis Powers be adopted at the Conference.
He has sent a personal message to that effect by courier to the Acting
President of Argentina and he is presently using all of Brazil's very
great influence in Chile in order to bring the Chilean Government in
line. It is not too much to say that had it not been for the strong and
helpful position taken by President Vargas and by Aranha four of the
other South American Republics would probably have drifted in the
direction of Argentina.

Last night President Vargas sent for me and after I had expressed
my deep appreciation of all that he had been doing to cooperate with
us he said that as I knew the decisions of his Government had been taken
and that the decisions were final. He continued that as Aranha had told
me earlier in the evening the latter had received during the day letters
addressed to him on [from] the German, Italian, and Japanese Ambassadors. These letters, whose texts I had seen stated, bluntly, in the case

of the German Ambassador and in a more veiled fashion in the case of the Japanese and Italian Ambassadors that if Brazil undertook to break diplomatic relations she could anticipate a state of war with the Axis Powers. (The letters were regarded as personal by the Brazilian Government and they are therefore anxious that no publicity should be given to their contents as yet.)

President Vargas then went on to say that the decision reached by the Brazilian Government implied inevitably that she would soon be actually at war. He said that the responsibility which he had assumed on behalf of the Brazilian people was very great. He said that it was peculiarly great because of the fact that notwithstanding all his efforts during the past 18 months to obtain at least a minimum of war supplies from the United States I myself knew what the result of his effort had been. He said that he felt that in view of the present circumstances he could depend upon you better than anyone else to understand his crucial difficulties. He went on to say that obviously Brazil could not be treated as a small Central American power which would be satisfied with the stationing of American troops upon its territory, but that Brazil rather has a right to be regarded by the United States as a friend and ally and as entitled to be furnished under the Lend-Lease Act with planes, tanks, and coast artillery sufficient to enable the Brazilian Army to defend at least in part those regions of northeastern Brazil whose defense is as vitally necessary for the United States as for Brazil herself.

In view of the nature of the conversation I regarded it as inexpedient to take up with the President the issue of the stationing of United States forces in northeastern Brazil in line with the understanding which I reached with General Marshall before I left Washington. Personally I have no doubt that this issue can be met successfully and that the Brazilian Government will agree thereto provided the Brazilian Army is given at least a minimum of material requested by President Vargas.

The conversation I had with the President was at a large gathering and I could only speak with him for a few moments. He has asked me to come to see him alone tomorrow, Monday, evening at 6 o'clock. I should like to be specifically authorized by you to state in the course of that conversation that I have communicated directly with you and that you have authorized me to say to him as Chief Executive of one great American nation to the Chief Executive of another great American nation and also as a personal friend that if the President will give me a list of the minimum requirements needed urgently by the Brazilian Army for the proper protection of northeastern Brazil you will give orders that the items contained in that list will be made available to the Brazilian Government at the first possible moment subject only to the exigencies of the present defense requirements of the United States of America and to any subsequent modifications that may later be agreed upon by the United States and Brazilian General Staffs.

As I know you will appreciate the issue involved is one of the highest national importance. . . . Like all armies, the Brazilian High Command is not inclined to be enthusiastic about getting into war if they have none of the basic elements for defense. If they are not promptly given the necessary assurances and if they are not able to see with their own eyes before long some concrete evidences of help coming, exactly that kind of a situation which the Nazis could use to their best advantage will be created.

The problem is one of such critical importance that I have felt it necessary to bring it to your attention immediately. I shall deeply appreciate it if you can let me have a favorable reply before my interview with President Vargas tomorrow evening.

Welles

The Ambassador in Brazil (Berle) to the Secretary of State
Rio de Janeiro, July 26, 1945.

Sir: I have the honor to report on the Naval Staff Conversations had between the United States and Brazil, which are embodied in a secret document dated April 15, 1945 from the Commander of the South Atlantic Force (Admiral Munroe) to the Commander-in-Chief of the United States Fleet and Chief of Naval Operations, together with its annexes. Further dispatches follow with respect to the conversations covering the ground forces and the air forces.

These Staff Conversations were conducted entirely between the officers of the Navy, without intervention of the Embassy. The Department is therefore clearly in a position to take any view which it chooses. The text of the Staff Conversations is presumably available to the Department in Washington through the Navy.

(1) Form: The form of the paper resulting from the Naval Staff Conversations is an official statement by the Brazilian Ministry of Marine as to what Brazil considers necessary for her post-war naval needs. Approval by the President of Brazil is taken, by the Navy, to mean that Brazil considers the plan feasible within her economy, and that Brazil will endeavor to maintain the proposed naval force at an effective level. For the purpose of this report, these assumptions are taken as correct.

(2) Political theory: The American naval officers based their suggestions on the assumption that "it is the desire of the United States that Brazil be able to play a strong and cooperative role in the maintenance of hemispherical defense as a component of post-war world order, thereby relieving the United States of the military burden and political embarrassment of playing this role directly in South America." I believe that the last phrase is open to some question. It implies that Brazil will be placed navally in a position to maintain peace substantially by herself in South America as well as to take her part in hemispheric defense. Certainly the Brazilian Naval General Staff wishes this. The size of the program projected supports this implication. The sense of the inter-American agreements do not contemplate anyone as a senior enforcement agency, but rather assumes that there is to be a cooperative enforcement of peace and a cooperative hemispheric defense. Nevertheless Brazil, as the largest South American country, necessarily will take primary rank in view of her superiority in size,

resources and possibly ultimate strength. . . .

(3) <u>Organization</u>: The organization envisaged is a continuing Naval Mission upon the existing contract basis, which, however, is to be enlarged through the assignment, on non-contract status, of specially qualified officers and men needed for training requirements. This personnel is to report to the Chief of Naval Mission, which is to be one of three such missions, the other two being an Army training mission and an Air training mission. It is contemplated that the senior members of these three missions will sit on the Joint United States-Brazil Military Commission.

This is sound organization as far as it goes; but there is the distinct danger that the American Section of the Commission would undertake to carry on foreign relations as well as military training. This Embassy has had a series of Army and Navy officers who not only have carried on direct relations with the Ministries of War, Navy and Air, but who also ask for and occasionally get direct relations with the President. In time of war this might be permissible. In time of peace it is not; and a civilian officer of the Embassy should at all times sit with the Military Commission. The Military or Naval Attachés will not do, since they are fundamentally reporting to their Departments. There is no point in duplicating the existing situation in which the Military Attaché, responsible as such to the Embassy, is also Chief of the Military Commission, in which position he appears to have independent jurisdiction. As long as the Naval Mission contemplated by the Staff Conversations, either acting by itself, or acting as a part of the Military Commission, is sticking to training, of course no difficulty arises. But these missions have a habit of extending their scope of operations, as we know from our experience with the Theater Commanders. To contemplate such a situation as a continuing and permanent part of the peace-time American machinery in Brazil would obviously be out of line.

The Naval Mission, like its companion Army and Air Missions, therefore should be required to report to the Embassy as well as to their respective Departments, and a civilian member of the Embassy should be required to cover it and the other two missions; and also the proposed American Section of the United States-Brazil Military Commission. In this connection, the Department should review the so-called Political Military Agreement of May 1942 to assure itself that the functions therein set forth are appropriately defined on a peacetime as well as a war-time basis.

(4) <u>Size</u> of <u>fleet:</u> The Brazilian Naval General Staff proposes that the United States shall make available to Brazil a number of vessels which are listed in paragraph 6 of a memorandum from the Chief of the Naval General Staff to the Minister of Marine and dated at Rio de Janeiro on February 21, 1945. This is attached to the report of the Staff Conversations. The principal items consist of two battleships of the <u>Nevada</u> class; two light aircraft carriers of the <u>Independence</u> class; four cruisers of the <u>Cleveland</u> class; fifteen destroyers; nine submarines, and a variety of auxiliary craft. The Staff Conversations do not suggest how these ships are to be paid for; but there is no question in my mind that the Brazilians hoped that they would be turned over either on Lend-Lease or on a nominal price basis. The American naval officers continuously refrained from making a recommendation.

(a) The fleet thus proposed, if Brazil could effectively operate it (which is questionable now) would make the Brazilian Navy incontestably the strongest naval force in South America, and substantially capable (assuming organization) of patrolling the East Coast of South America and the bulk of the South Atlantic. Such a fleet could not be challenged from within the hemisphere; equally, it would be wholly ineffective against challenge from a strong power from without the hemisphere. It could, if organized, be of considerable assistance to the United States in the event that the hemisphere were attacked from outside, by relieving our country of part of the patrol duty in the South Atlantic. My impression is that the aid is apparent rather than real, and that actually the United States would have to send technicians, officers, et cetera, to organize, supply and handle the fleet. Probably the United States Navy could do this work better under the American flag than under the Brazilian. The possession of such a fleet would give to Brazil a naval prestige which would be a solid political advantage on the assumption that Brazil continues her historic policy of collaboration with the United States. For the foreseeable future this assumption is warranted. It is conceivable, however, that a different situation might arise, and in such case the Brazilian naval force would become an embarrassment. Actually, I strongly doubt whether the Brazilian Navy could handle a force of this size in the immediate future. My recommendation would be that a force of this size be left as a possible ideal to be attained at some future date; but that the program for realizing it be left fluid, and that a considerably less program be envisaged for the immediate future. One cruiser of the Cleveland class might be scheduled for turnover to the Brazilian Navy as and when it becomes sufficiently clear that the Brazilian Navy is able to handle it, with possible turnover on a similar basis of a second cruiser, and later, one light aircraft carrier. The destroyer program should also be appropriately cut down. Even to realize this, in my judgment, would be a matter of at least three or four years.

(b) My reason for being skeptical about the battleships likewise proceeds from a doubt whether in any foreseeable period of time the Brazilian Navy would be able to defend a battleship against an air attack even from an inferior power. In practice, battleships of the Nevada class could only be used as floating batteries requiring a possible enemy to deploy more force in the event of a landing. In a naval engagement it is highly questionable whether they could stand up. It has still to be demonstrated that the Brazilian Navy could carry on the maintenance of as complicated and formidable a piece of machinery as even a Nevada class battleship.

(c) The foregoing two paragraphs are based on the assumption that the United States could find some way of turning over these ships to Brazil for nothing or on a nominal price basis. Actually, in my judgment, Brazil would do well not to spend any great amount of money in acquiring a fleet, beyond perhaps a single cruiser. She could better rely on cooperation with the United States Navy, which will be able to detach a naval force for purposes of assisting in maintaining hemispheric peace. In case of defense against attack from outside the hemisphere, the United States would have to expand its entire Navy as rapidly as possible to cover all contingencies. The money and effort used in organizing a naval force at this point in Brazilian history would be infinitely better spent on putting in an internal transport system, and building and maintaining public schools. If another war test actually comes, this particular kit of naval machinery will probably be out of date; and Brazil's real reliance will then have to be on a wider sector of literate and trained people, and a better ability to mobilize her internal resources. Meantime, she can safely rely on the United States Navy for her defense. In my judgement, this would be sound policy. For this reason, I should not favor a too rapid development of the Brazilian Navy if this involves any great expense to Brazil.

(d) The foregoing observations apply in considerable measure to the maintenance cost contemplated by proposed increase of the Brazilian Navy.

(5) Naval bases: While I am dubious about the size of the fleet, quite different considerations apply to the naval base program. Paragraph 9 of the memorandum of February 21, 1945 proposes six naval bases and an arsenal, namely, a Main Base at Rio de Janeiro; the Ganchos Base at Santa Catharina; the Rio Grande Base for small craft; the Natal Base with auxiliary installations at Recife; the Bahía Base; the Pará Base located near Belém, and an arsenal at Ladario, to serve the Paraguay River Force.

(a) These bases would be of solid use in the event of operations of any kind whether to maintain peace in the hemisphere or to defend the hemisphere from attack from without; but their principal use would probably be to assist operations of the United States Navy. In case of real trouble, if Brazil had not built these bases, we should probably have to build them for Brazil, for joint United States-Brazilian use. I should recommend the implementation of the Staff Conversations through creation as recommended of a special commission to organize the definite projects for the bases, and the rendering by the United States of all possible assistance in constructing, maintaining and setting up these bases upon the understanding that they would be available for joint operations in case of war, and for periodical maneuver and practice operations in time of peace.

(6) Training: The proposed plan of joint United States and Brazilian training of technicians should, in my judgement, go forward, though on a restricted basis, substantially along the lines indicated.

(7) Cost: The cost of putting the program into effect is estimated roughly by the Brazilian Naval General Staff at Cr.$799.863.280,00, covering three years. This is assumed to include everything except any payment for the fleet itself. The estimate looks low to me. Obviously if the plan were put into effect slowly, annual costs would be correspondingly reduced.

On the other hand, the Brazilian Naval General Staff estimates that construction of all bases plus training of personnel would result in an additional cost of Cr.$133.375.000,00 (approximately 6 and one half million dollars) roughly for each of the years 1945, 1946, and 1947. Alternatively, by proceeding with the program more slowly, and dividing the bases into groups, the money could be spread out so that about Cr.$70.000.000,00 a year (approximately 3 and one half million dollars) could keep the program moving forward. I should recommend the latter method.

Neither the Navy, the Army or the Air Force representatives considered economics very much in their Staff Conversations. They figured, as military men usually do, that providing the money was the job of a civilian government which would have to judge its own ability in that regard. My own feeling is that a limited amount of money for a base program is probably well spent, all things considered. Additional sums suggested for fleet development and maintenance would be of more solid military advantage both to the United States and Brazil if they were put into developing the transport and economic and human resources of Brazil. For a country which has at the moment a total national income of less than 3 billion dollars, a total additional expenditure for Navy alone which the Naval Staff estimates at Cr.$799.000.000,00 and probably would run to not less than Cr.$1,000.000.000,00 (i.e. $50,000,000) exclusive of any additional cost of the ships themselves, is a huge sum. This does not take account of the fact that continued maintenance would have to be provided for and aircraft carriers are especially expensive to maintain. Yet naval expense is only a fraction of the total program with the bills for air and ground forces still to come in.

(8) General policy: I feel that the sound policy for Brazil is to have a reasonably capable naval police force, with enough large ships (one or two cruisers) to maintain her prestige; but that her real defense at this point in the world's history should be her virtual alliance with the United States within the framework of the inter-American arrangements envisaged by the Act of Chapultepec and presently to be carried forward into a definitive treaty. This policy is peculiarly applicable to the Navy, since the United States will at all times maintain a powerful mobile fleet, which will be more efficient in American hands than in Brazilian. The money which might be used to provide a sixth rate fleet, will tend to impoverish and weaken the country. That same amount of money spent in educating Brazilians and developing transport, industry and resources, will strengthen the country. It is probable that if and when a test comes, the Brazilian naval force would have to be thoroughly reorganized anyhow in the light of new weapons and new methods.

The existing measures should accordingly be trimmed to a manageable program providing for building of the bases, limited fleet additions for patrol and police purposes, a social training program, and maintenance of firm and continuing relations enabling the United States Fleet to move to the defense of Brazil, or to work in conjunction with Brazil for defense of the hemisphere, or maintenance of peace within the hemisphere, as the case may be.

(9) The Brazilian naval expectations have undoubtedly been greatly raised by the Staff Conversations themselves, and even more by the very unfortunate speech of Admiral Ingram, which was taken to be a promise of full delivery of the entire amount of Navy materiél. This speech was unauthorized. Admiral Ingram is presently a Brazilian hero for having promised the Brazilians a Navy free of charge.

Yet we have to cope with the results. To throw overboard the Naval

Staff Conversations now would undoubtedly create a very considerable
crisis. I should therefore recommend that the Department and the Navy,
retaining the program as an ideal, propose measures designed to make
progress toward realizing it without commitments as to time, accompanied by an understanding with the Brazilian Naval Staff that the program be subject to review and revision in the light of new weapons and
new conditions.

Respectfully yours,   A.A. Berle, Jr.

EXIT VARGAS, TRAGICALLY (1954)

Getúlio Vargas was twice forced out of the Brazilian presidency by action of the military, first in October, 1945, and second and finally on August 24, 1954. On the first occasion he accepted the irresistable action with grace and resilience. The latter quality permitted his return to politics and to the presidency in 1950. But by his second round in office he could not approach its responsibilities with the élan and agility he had earlier displayed, especially between 1937 and 1945. Nor could he cope with the progressive economic and political deterioration that preceded the army coup of August, 1954. By that time the resilience was gone and his only answer was suicide.

He left an emotional and cryptic suicide letter or "political testament" (the authenticity of which was subsequently questioned). It was published on August 25, 1954, the day following his suicide, by the New York Times; ©1954 by the New York Times Company. Reprinted by permission.

Once more the forces and interests against the people are newly coordinated and raised against me. They do not accuse me, they insult me; they do not fight me, they slander me and do not give me the right of defense. They need to drown my voice and halt my actions so that I can no longer continue to defend, as I always have defended, the people and principally the humble.

I follow the destiny that is imposed on me. After years of domination and looting by international economic and financial groups, I made myself chief of an unconquerable revolution. I began the work of liberation and I instituted a regime of social liberty. I had to resign. I returned to govern on the arms of the people.

A subterranean campaign of international groups joined with national groups revolting against the regime of workers' guarantees. The law of excess profits was stopped in Congress. Hatreds were unchanged against the justice of a revision of minimum salaries.

I wished to create national liberty by developing our riches through Petrobras [the government oil development company] and a wave of agitation clouded its beginnings. Electrobras [the government hydroelectric development agency] was hindered almost to despair. They do not wish the workers to be free. They do not wish the people to be independent.

I assumed the Government during an inflationary spiral that was destroying the value of work. Profits of foreign enterprises reached 500 per cent yearly. In declarations of goods that we import there existed frauds of more than $100,000,000.

I saw the coffee crises increase the value of our principal product. We attempted to defend its price and the reply was a violent pressure upon our economy to the point of being obliged to surrender.

I have fought month to month, day to day, hour to hour, resisting a constant aggression, unceasingly bearing it all in silence, forgetting all and renouncing myself to defend the people that now fall abandoned. I cannot give you more than my blood. If the birds of prey wish the blood of anybody, they wish to continue sucking that of the Brazilian people.

I offer my life in the holocaust. I choose this means to be with you always. When they humiliate you, you will feel my soul suffering at your side. When hunger beats at your door, you will feel in your chests the energy for the fight for yourselves and your children. When they humiliate you, you feel in my grief the force for reaction.

My sacrifice will maintain you united, and my name will be your battle flag. Each drop of my blood will be an immortal call to your conscience and will maintain a holy vibration for resistance.

To hatred, I respond with pardon. And to those who think they have defeated me, I reply with my victory. I was the slave of the people and today I free myself for eternal life. But this people to which I was a slave no longer will be a slave to anyone. My sacrifice will remain forever in your soul and my blood will be the price of your ransom.

I fought against the looting of Brazil. I fought against the looting of the people. I have fought bare-breasted. The hatred, infamy, and calumny did not beat down my spirit. I gave you my life. Now I offer my death. Nothing remains. Serenely I take the first step on the road to eternity and I leave life to enter history.

EXIT QUADROS, CRYPTICALLY (1961)

Jânio Quadros had served quite capably as mayor of São Paulo city and as governor of São Paulo state prior to his election to the presidency in 1960 and his inauguration at the end of January, 1961. As president, however, he did not display the same qualities of leadership and political acumen that he had demonsuicide of Vargas came the equally dramatic resignation of Quadros from the presidency. Like Vargas he left a letter of extenuation, even somewhat similar in tone.

The letter was published in the New York Times on August 26, 1961. © 1961 by the New York Times Company. Reprinted by permission.

On this date and by this communication I am leaving with the Minister of Justice the reasons for the act in which I hereby resign my post as President of the Republic.

I have been beaten by forces against me and so I leave the Government. In the last seven months I have carried out my duty. I have done so night and day, always working harder and harder without any rancor against anyone. But unfortunately all my efforts were in vain to lead this nation in the direction of its true economic and political freedom, which was the only way to effective social progress which this generous people are so much entitled to.

I wanted Brazil for Brazilians and because [I did] I had to face and fight corruption, lies and cowardliness, whose only goals are to subject the general needs of the nation to some ambitious groups and individuals from inside and also from outside.

However, I feel crushed. Terrible forces came forward to fight me and to defame me by all their means with the excuse that they were only trying to collaborate. Had I remained at my post I would share no longer the confidence and peace necessary to carry on with my duties. I believe that I would not even be able to maintain the public peace.

Here I call a halt with my thoughts turned toward the people, the students, and the workers and also to the whole Brazilian community. Here I close this page of my life and of the national history. I have enough courage to do so.

In leaving the government I want to make an appeal and express my gratitude.

My gratitude to those who have helped me inside and outside my administration and especially to the armed forces whose conduct and behaviour I wish to proclaim at this very moment.

My appeal is that order and respect should be maintained from one and all.

This is the only way we shall have the necessary dignity to inherit our Christian destiny.

I return now to my work as lawyer and teacher. Let us all work. ere are many ways of serving our nation.

CONTEMPORARY MILITARISM (1969)

As noted in a preceding document, militarism has been in central seats of power at various times in Brazilian history. Never has it been more evident nor more heavy-handed than it has been since an army coup ousted President Goulart in 1964.

The constitution in 1937, as illustrated by a previous document, concentrated governmental power, but with a difference from that currently in effect. The Vargas law conceded great authority to executive, and especially presidential, hands. The constitution of 1967, as amended October 17, 1969, was, as the earlier one was not, a product of the military rather than the civilian sector. In subtle, and sometimes not so subtle, ways it conferred great power and prestige on military institutions and officers. Illustrative extracts are given in the following document.

This English translation of the 1967 (1969) constitution was published by the Organization of American States in 1970.

Section V

National Security

Article 86. Every natural or juridical person is responsible for national security, within the limits defined by law.

Article 87. The National Security Council is the organ of the highest level in providing direct advice to the president of the republic for the formulation and execution of national security policy.

Article 88. The National Security Council is presided over by the president of the republic, and the vice president of the republic and all the minister of state shall participate in it ex officio.

Sole paragraph. The law shall regulate the organizations, competence, and functioning of the Council and may admit others to it as ex officio or special members.

Article 89. The National Security Council shall have the power:

I. To establish the permanent national objectives and the bases for national policy;

II. To study, in the domestic and foreign sphere, the matters of importance to national security.

III. To indicate the areas that are indispensable to the national security and the municipalities considered to be important to it;

IV. To give prior consent, in the areas indispensable to the national security, for:

    a. Concession of lands, opening of transportation routes, and installation of means of communication;

    b. Construction of bridges, international roads, and airfields; and

    c. Establishment or operation of any industry affecting the national security;

  V. To modify or cancel the concessions or authorizations referred to in the preceding item; and

 VI. To grant permission for the operation of organs or delegations of foreign labor union entities, as well as to authorize the affiliation of national labor union organizations with such entities.

Sole paragraph. The law shall indicate the municipalities of importance to the national security and the areas indispensable to it and shall regulate their ulitization, ensuring the predominance of Brazilian capital and workers in the industries located therein.

Section VI

The Armed Forces

Article 90. The armed forces, consisting of the Navy, the Army, and the Air Force, are permanent and regular national institutions, organized on the basis of rank and discipline, under the supreme authority of the president of the republic and within the limits of the law.

Article 91. It is the mission of the armed forces, which are essential to the execution of the national security policy, to defend the country and to guarantee the constituted powers, and law and order.

Sole paragraph. The president of the republic is responsible for the direction of war policy and the selection of the principal commanders.

Article 92. All Brazilians are obligated to military service or other duties necessary to the national security, under the terms and penalties of the law.

Sole paragraph. Women and clergymen are exempt from military service in peacetime but are subject to other duties the law may assign to them.

Article 93. Commissions, with the advantages, prerogatives, and duties inherent therein, are fully guaranteed not only to active and reserve officers but also to retired officers.

Paragraph 1. Military rank, posts, and uniforms are the exclusive right of active, reserve, or retired members of the armed forces. Uniforms shall be used in the manner the law determines.

Paragraph 2. An officer of the armed forces shall lose his post and commission only if he is declared unworthy of or incompatible with the rank of officer, by decision of a permanent military court, in time of peace, or of a special court, in time of war.

Paragraph 3. A member of the armed forces sentenced by a civil or military court to a punishment restricting individual liberty for more than two years, by final condemnatory sentence, shall be brought to trial as provided in the preceding paragraph.

Paragraph 4. A member of the armed forces on active duty appointed to any permanent public position not connected with his career shall immediately be transferred to the reserve, with the rights and duties defined by law.

Paragraph 5. The law shall regulate the situation of a member of the armed forces on active duty who is appointed to any temporary, civilian, nonelective public position, including a position with an autonomous agency. While he is in the service, he shall remain attached to the corresponding roster and may be promoted only for seniority, and his time of service shall be counted only for that promotion and transfer to inactive duty, which shall take place after two years of separation, continuous or not, as provided by law.

Paragraph 6. While he is receiving remuneration from the position referred to in the preceding paragraph, a member of the armed forces on active duty shall not be entitled to his regular salary and benefits, but his right to choose which salary he wishes to receive shall be assured.

Paragraph 7. The age limits and other conditions for the transfer of members of the armed forces to retirement shall be established by law.

Paragraph 8. Retirement benefits shall be adjusted if, because of a change in the purchasing power of money, the salaries of members of the armed forces on active duty are changed; with the exception of cases provided for by law, retirement benefits shall not exceed the remuneration received by a member of the armed forces on active duty in the position or rank corresponding to that of his benefits.

Paragraph 9. The prohibition against receiving more than one retirement benefit shall not be applied to members of the military reserve forces and to retired members, with respect to the holding of an elective office, with respect to performing the function of teaching or of a task to which they are appointed, or with respect to a contract for provision of technical or specialized services.

Section V

Military Courts and Judges

Article 127. The Superior Military Court and such lower courts and judges as are established by law are organs of military justice.

Article 128. The Superior Military Court shall be composed of fifteen judges, appointed for life by the president of the republic after their selection has been approved by the federal Senate, three of them being selected from among active Navy flag officers, four from among active general officers of the Army, three from among active general officers of the Air Force, and five from among civilians.

Paragraph 1. The civilian judges shall be citizens over thirty-five years of age, freely selected by the president of the republic as follows:
    a.   Three of them being of recognized juridical learning and high moral character, with more than ten years of court experience; and
    b.   Two of them being judges or members of the public ministry of military justice, of proven juridical learning.

Paragraph 2. The military and civilian judges of the Superior Military Court shall receive remuneration equal to that of the judges of the federal Court of Appeals.

Paragraph 3. In exceptional cases, general officers of the reserve, of the first class, may be appointed justices of the Superior Military Court.

Article 129. The military courts shall have the power to try and to judge military and related personnel for military crimes defined by law.

Paragraph 1. This special jurisdiction may be extended to civilians in cases provided for by law, for the repression of crimes against national security or the military institutions.

Paragraph 2. The Superior Military Court shall have the power to try and to judge, in the first instance, the state governors and their secretaries, for the crimes referred to in paragraph 1.

Paragraph 3. The law shall regulate the application of the penalties of military legislation.

Chapter II

Political Rights

Article 147. Brazilians over eighteen years of age registered as prescribed by law shall be voters.

Paragraph 1. Registration and voting are obligatory for Brazilians of both sexes, subject to the exceptions established by law.

Paragraph 2. A member of the armed forces may register if he is an officer, officer-candidate, midshipman, warrant officer, noncommissioned officer, or student in a military school of higher education for officer training.

Paragraph 3. The following may not register as voters:

a. Illiterate persons;
b. Those who do not know how to express themselves in the national language;
c. Those who are deprived, temporarily or permanently, of political rights.

Article 148. Suffrage shall be universal and voting shall be direct and secret, except in the cases where it is otherwise provided in this Constitution; political parties shall have complete or partial proportional representation, in the manner established by law.

Article 149. The suspension or loss of political rights may be declared, with the person who is the object of the action being assured ample defense.

Paragraph 1. The president of the republic shall decree the loss of political rights:

a. In the cases of Article 146, items I and II, and sole paragraph;
b. For refusal, based on religious, philosophical, or political convictions, to perform a duty or service required of Brazilians in general; or
c. For acceptance of a foreign decoration or title of nobility that implies restriction of the right of citizenship or duty toward the Brazilian state.

Paragraph 2. Loss or suspension of political rights shall result from a judicial decision:

a. In the case of Article 146, item III;
b. For absolute civil incapacity; or

c. For criminal conviction, as long as its effects may last.

Paragraph 3. A supplementary law shall stipulate regarding the specification of political rights, the enjoyment, the exercise, the loss of suspension of all or any of them and the cases in which they may be reinstated and the conditions therefor.

Article 150. Persons who may not be registered may not be elected to office.

Paragraph 1. Members of the armed forces may be elected to office, under the following conditions:

    a. A member of the armed forces who has less than five years of service shall, when he becomes a candidate for elective office, be excluded from active service;

    b. A member of the armed forces on active duty who has five or more years of service shall, when he becomes a candidate for elective office, be removed temporarily from active service and attached in order to take care of private interest.

    c. A member of the armed forces not excluded, if elected, shall at the time when he is given his credentials of election, be transferred to the reserve as provided by law.

Paragraph 2. The eligibility to which reference is made in subparagraphs a and b of the preceding paragraph does not depend, for members of the armed forces on active duty, on affiliation with a political party, which may at present be or in the future become a legal requirement.

Article 151. A supplementary law shall establish the cases of ineligibility and the time periods when this shall cease, with a view to the preservation:

    I. Of the democratic system;

    II. Of administrative honesty;

    III. Of the normality and legitimacy of elections, aimed against abuse in the exercise of a directly or indirectly administrered government function, position, or employment, or against abuse of financial power; and

    IV. Of morality in the exercise of the office, taking into consideration the experience of the candidate prior thereto.

Sole paragraph. The following standards shall be observed, and are to take force at once, in the preparation of the supplementary law:

    a. The ineligibility of persons who have held the office of president or vice president of the republic, of governor or vice governor, of prefect or vice prefect, for any period of time in the immediately preceding term;

    b. The ineligibility of the person who within the six months preceding the election succeeded the office holder or has served as substitute for the latter, in any of the offices indicated in subparagraph a;

    c. The ineligibility of the actual interim office holder occupying a position or function the exercise of which might have the influence of disturbing the normality of the elections or casting doubt on their legitimacy, unless the person concerned removes himself from the position or the function within the period set by law, which shall not be more than six nor less than two months preceding the election;

d. The ineligibility, in the territory of the jurisdiction of the office holder, of the spouse and the relatives to the third degree of consanguinity or affinity, or relatives by adoption, of the president of the republic, the governor of a state or territory, a prefect or a person who substituted for any of the foregoing within the six months preceding the election; and

e. The compulsory nature of electoral domicile in the state or in the municipality for a period of between one and two years, determined according to the nature of the office or function.

Chapter III

Political Parties

Article 152. The organization, functioning, and dissolution of political parites shall be regulated by federal law, the following principles being observed:

I.   A representative and democratic system, based on plurality of parties and on guarantee of the fundamental rights of man;

II.   Juridical personality, through registration of bylaws;

III. Continuing activities, within a program approved by the Superior Electoral Court, and without any connection of any nature with the action of foreign governments, entities, or parties;

IV.   Financial control;

V.   Party discipline;

VI.   National scope, without prejudice to the deliberative functions of local executive committees;

VII. Requirement of five percent of the electorate that voted in the last general election for the Chamber of Deputies, distributed in at least seven states, with a minimum of seven percent in each of them.

VIII. Prohibition of coalitions of parties.

Sole paragraph. An office held in the federal Senate, the Chamber of Deputies, the legislative assemblies, or the municipal councils shall be lost by a person who, by attitudes or by vote, opposes the directives legitimately established by the organs of party leadership or who leaves the party under whose emblem he was elected. The loss of office shall be decreed by electoral justice, upon the representation of the party, and the right to full defense shall be assured.

APPENDICES

RULERS OF BRAZIL SINCE 1808

State of Brazil in the Kingdom of Portugal and the Algarves

João, Prince of Brazil, Regent   January 22, 1808

United Kingdom of Portugal, Brazil, and the Algarves

João, Prince of Brazil, Regent   December 15, 1815
João VI, King   March 20, 1816
Pedro, Prince Royal, Regent   April 26, 1821

Empire

Pedro I   September 7, 1822
Regency   April 7, 1831
Pedro II   July 23, 1840

Republic

Deodoro da Fonseca   November 15, 1889
Floriano Peixoto   November 23, 1891
Prudente José de Moraes Barros   November 15, 1894
Manoel Ferras de Campos Salles   November 15, 1898
Francisco de Paula Rodrigues Alves   November 15, 1902
Affonso Augusto Moreira Penna   November 15, 1906
Nilo Peçanha   June 14, 1909
Hermes da Fonseca   November 15, 1910
Wenceslau Braz Pereira Gomes   November 15, 1914
Delfim Moreira da Costa Ribeiro   November 15, 1918
Epitácio Pessôa   July 28, 1919
Artur da Silva Bernardes   November 15, 1922
Washington Luís Pereira de Sousa   November 15, 1926
Getúlio Vargas   November 4, 1930
José Linhares   October 29, 1945
Eurico Gaspar Dutra   January 31, 1946
Getúlio Vargas   January 31, 1951
João Café Filho   August 24, 1954
Carlos Luz   November 8, 1955
Nereu Ramos   November 11, 1955
Juscelino Kubitschek   January 31, 1956
Janio da Silva Quadros   January 31, 1961

João Goulart	September 7, 1961
Ranieri Mazzili	April 2, 1964
Humberto Castelo Branco	April 11, 1964
Artur da Costa e Silva	March 15, 1967
<u>Junta</u>	August 30, 1969
Emílio Garrastazú Médici	October 7, 1969

EMINENT BRAZILIANS

(Exclusive of Rulers)

Castro Alves (1847-1871), author, abolitionist
Jorge Amado (1912-   ), author
José Bonifacio de Andrada e Silva (1765-1838), statesman, geologist
Oswaldo Aranha (1894-1960), statesman, president of UN General Assembly, 1947-49
Francisco de Assis Chateaubriand (1891-   ), publisher
Ruy Barbosa (1849-1923), statesman, jurist
Vital Brasil (1865-1950), physician, developer of the Butantan Institute
Emiliano di Cavalcanti (1897-   ), painter
Lucio Costa (1902-   ), architect
Oswaldo Cruz (1872-1917), physician, public health pioneer
Euclides da Cunha (1866-1909), author (Os Sertões)
Antônio Gonçalves Dias (1824-1864), poet
Oscar Lorenzo Fernandes (1897-1948), composer
Gilberto Freyre (1900-   ), author, sociologist
Bruno Giorgio (1905-   ), sculptor
Carlos Gomes (1836-1896), composer
Camargo Guarnieri (1907-   ), composer
Luís Alves de Lima, Duke of Caxias (1803-1880), general
José Lins do Rego (1900-1959), author
Antônio Francisco Lisboa (Aleijadinho) (1730-1814), architect
Joaquim Marques Lisboa, Marquis of Tamandaré (1807-1897), naval hero
Joaquim Maria Machado de Assis (1839-1908), novelist (Dom Casmurro)
Francisco Mignone (1897-   ), composer
Joaquim Nabuco (1849-1910), abolitionist
Alberto Nepomuceno (1846-1920), opera composer
Oscar Niemeyer (1907-   ), architect
Guiomar Novaës (1895-   ) concert pianist
Manoel de Oliveira Lima (1867-1928), historian
Candido Portinari (1903-1962), painter
Sylvio Romero (1851-1914), essayist
Candido Rondon (1865-1957), general, explorer, Indianist
Alberto Santos Dumont (1837-1932), aviation pioneer
Bidu Sayão (1902-   ), operatic soprano
José Maria de Silva Paranhos, Baron of Rio Branco (1847-1912), foreign minister
Irineu Evangelista de Souza, Baron of Mauá (1813-1889), industrialist
Francisco Adolfo Varnhagen, Viscount of Porto Seguro (1816-1878), historian
Erico Verissimo (1905-   ), author

José Verissimo (1857-1916), essayist
Heitor Villa-Lobos (1887-1959), composer

AREA AND POPULATION

STATE AND CAPITAL	AREA (sq. miles)	POPULATION , 1970 (provisional)
(North)		
Rondônia (terr., Porto Velho)	93,815	113,659
Acre (Rio Branco)	58,899	216,200
Amazonas (Manaus)	607,876	955,194
Roraima (terr., Boa Vista)	88,820	40,915
Pará (Belem)	482,805	2,161,316
Amapá (terr., Macapá)	54,147	114,687
(Northeast)		
Maranhão (São Luís)	126,908	2,997,576
Piauí (Teresina)	96,861	1,680,954
Ceará (Fortaleza)	58,143	4,366,970
Rio Grande do Norte (Natal)	20,464	1,552,158
Paraíba (João Pessoa)	21,760	2,384,615
Pernambuco (Recife)	37,936	5,166,554
Alagoas (Maceió)	10,704	1,589,605
Fernando de Noronha (terr.)	10	1,239
Sergipe (Aracajú)	8,490	901,618
Bahia (Salvador)	220,556	7,508,779
(Southeast)		
Minas Gerais (Belo Horizonte)	226,709	11,497,574
Espírito Santo (Vitória)	17,600	1,600,305
Rio de Janeiro (Niteroi)	16,564	4,746,848
Guanabara (Rio de Janeiro)	523	4,252,009
São Paulo (São Paulo)	95,689	17,775,889
(South)		
Paraná (Curitiba)	77,028	6,936,743
Santa Catarina (Florianópolis)	37,050	2,903,360
Rio Grande do Sul (Porto Alegre)	108,923	6,670,382
(Central West)		
Mato Grosso (Cuiabá)	475,378	1,600,494
Goiás (Goiânia)	287,848	2,941,107
Federal District (Brasília)	2,244	538,351
BRAZIL	3,285,622	93,215,301

POPULATION IN THE RESPECTIVE NATIONAL CENSUSES

1872	10,112,061
1890	14,333,915
1900	17,318,556
1920	30,635,605
1940	41,236,315
1950	51,944,397
1960	70,119,071
1970	93,215,301

POPULATION OF PRINCIPAL CITIES, 1970

São Paulo	5,241,232
Rio de Janeiro	4,315,746
Belo Horizonte	1,126,368
Recife	1,070,078
Salvador	1,017,591
Porto Alegre	887,338
Belem	572,654
Fortaleza	529,933
Goiânia	370,619
Niteroi	297,720
Manaus	286,083
Brasília	277,005

BIBLIOGRAPHY

BIBLIOGRAPHY

Alexander, Robert J. Labor Relations in Argentina, Brazil, and Chile.
New York: McGraw-Hill, 1962.

Azevedo, Fernando de. Brazilian Culture: An Introduction to the Study of
Culture in Brazil. New York: Macmillan, 1950.

Azevedo, Thales de. Social Change in Brazil. Gainesville: University of
Florida Press, 1962.

Baer, Werner. Industrialization and the Economic Development of Brazil.
New Haven; Yale University Press, 1965.

Bello, José Maria. A History of the Republic, 1889-1964. Stanford: Stanford University Press, 1964.

Boxer, Charles. The Golden Age of Brazil. Berkeley: University of California Press, 1962.

Burns, E. Bradford. A History of Brazil. New York: Columbia University Press, 1970.

Burns, E. Bradford. Nationalism in Brazil. New York: Praeger, 1968.

Calógeras, João Pandiá. A History of Brazil. Chapel Hill: University of
North Carolina Press, 1939.

Camacho, J.A. Brazil, an Interim Assessment. London: Royal Institute of
International Affairs, 1954.

Cunha, Euclides da. Rebellion in the Backlands. Chicago: University of
Chicago Press, 1945.

Dulles, John W. F. Vargas of Brazil. Austin: University of Texas Press,
1967.

Ellison, Fred P. Brazil's New Novel. Berkeley: University of California
Press, 1954.

Fernandes, Floristan. The Negro in Brazilian Society. New York: Columbia University Press, 1969.

Freyre, Gilberto. The Mansions and the Shanties. New York: Knopf, 1963

Freyre, Gilberto. The Masters and the Slaves. New York: Knopf, 1956.

Freyre, Gilberto, New World in the Tropics: The Culture of Modern Brazil. New York: Knopf, 1959.

Furtado, Celso. The Economic Growth of Brazil. Berkeley: University of California Press, 1965.

Graham, Richard (ed.) A Century of Brazilian History since 1865: Issues and Problems. New York: Knopf, 1969.

Harding, Bertita. Amazon Throne. Indianapolis: Bobbs, Merrill, 1941

Haring, Clarence H. Empire in Brazil: A New World Experiment with Monarchy. Cambridge: Harvard University Press, 1958.

Hill, Lawrence F. (ed.) Brazil. Berkeley: University of California Press, 1947.

Horowitz, Irving L. Revolution in Brazil. New York: Dutton, 1964.

Hunnicutt, Benjamin H. Brazil, World Frontier. New York: Van Nostrand, 1949.

Marchant, Anyda. Viscount Mauá and the Empire of Brazil. Berkeley: University of California Press, 1965.

Morse, Richard M. From Community to Metropolis [São Paulo]. Gainesville: University of Florida Press, 1958.

Nash, Roy. The Conquest of Brazil. New York: Harcourt, Brace, 1926.

Normano, João F. Brazil: A Study of Economic Types. Chapel Hill: University of North Carolina Press, 1935.

Pierson, Donald. Negroes in Brazil: A Study of Race Contact at Bahia. Chicago: University of Chicago Press, 1942.

Putnam, Samuel. Marvelous Journey: Four Centuries of Brazilian Literature. New York: Knopf, 1948.

Reisky de Dubnic, Vladimir. Political Trends in Brazil. Washington: Public Affairs Press, 1968.

Rodrigues, José Honório. Brazil and Africa. Berkeley: University of California Press, 1965.

Rodrigues, José Honório. The Brazilians: Their Character and Aspirations. Austin: University of Texas Press, 1967.

Schurz, William L. Brazil: The Infinite Country. New York: Dutton, 1961.

Skidmore, Thomas E. Politics in Brazil, 1930-1964. New York: Oxford University Press, 1967.

Smith, T. Lynn. Brazil: People and Institutions. Baton Rouge: Louisiana State University Press, 1963.

Tavares de Sá, Hernane. The Brazilians: People of Tomorrow. New York: Day, 1947.

Vellinho, Moysés. Brazil South: Its Conquest and Settlement. New York: Knopf, 1968.

Verissimo, Erico. Brazilian Literature. New York: Macmillan, 1944.

Verissimo, Erico. Time and the Mind. New York: Macmillan, 1951.

Wagley, Charles. Race and Class in Rural Brazil. Paris: UNESCO, 1953.

Willems, Emilio. Followers of the New Faith: Culture Change and the Rise of Protestantism in Brazil and Chile. Nashville: Vanderbilt University Press, 1967.

Williams, Mary W. Dom Pedro the Magnanimous. Chapel Hill: University of North Carolina Press, 1937.

Young, Jordan M. The Brazilian Revolution of 1930 and the Aftermath. New Brunswick: Rutgers University Press, 1967.

NAME INDEX